GOD INCARNATE:
STORY AND BELIEF

GOD INCARNATE:
STORY AND BELIEF

---

edited by
A. E. HARVEY

LONDON
SPCK

1981

First published 1981

SPCK
Holy Trinity Church
Marylebone Road
London NW1 4DU

The authors retain the copyright of their contributions
© Anthony Harvey   James Barr   John Macquarrie   Rachel Trickett
Geza Vermes   Peter Hinchliff   Peter Baelz   1981

ACKNOWLEDGEMENTS

Scripture quotations are from the Revised Standard Version of the Bible,
copyrighted 1946 and 1952 by the Division of Christian Education of the
National Council of the Churches of Christ in the USA.

Thanks are due to Faber and Faber Ltd for permission to quote lines from
The Journey of the Magi by T. S. Eliot, and from *For the Time Being* by
W. H. Auden.

Line from *Christmas* by John Betjeman are reprinted by permission of
John Murray (Publishers) Ltd and Houghton Mifflin Co.

Printed and bound in Great Britain by
Mansell (Bookbinders) Limited
Witham, Essex

ISBN 0 281 03832 5

Contents

The Contributors

PETER BAELZ — Dean of Durham; formerly Regius Professor of Moral and Pastoral Theology in the University of Oxford

JAMES BARR — Regius Professor of Hebrew and Student of Christ Church, Oxford

ANTHONY HARVEY — University Lecturer in Theology and Fellow of Wolfson College, Oxford

PETER HINCHLIFF — Fellow and Chaplain of Balliol College, Oxford

JOHN MACQUARRIE — Lady Margaret Professor of Divinity and Canon of Christ Church, Oxford

RACHEL TRICKETT — Principal of St Hugh's College, Oxford

GEZA VERMES — Reader in Jewish Studies and Fellow of Wolfson College, Oxford

Preface

FOLLOWING the publication of *The Myth of God Incarnate*** in 1977, a small group of us who held teaching posts at Oxford began to meet regularly to discuss some of the issues raised by that book. It was not that we wished to offer an 'answer' to it, or to join in the chorus of protest which it had aroused; but we found that our own thinking was moving in directions which enabled us for the most part to express our convictions more positively than was possible (at least by the end of their argument) for the authors of *The Myth*.

Since each of us was a specialist in a different area of theology (and also, with the welcome addition to our number of Rachel Trickett, in literary criticism), we naturally approached our discussions from different angles; but we found that something of a common approach was emerging from the papers we read to each other, and that this was sufficient for us to feel we could make some contribution to the contemporary debate on the person and nature of Jesus Christ. These papers certainly do not represent an agreed statement: we could hardly claim to be professional academics if we did not differ among ourselves! But we have subjected each one to intensive discussion, and each of us is happy to be associated with a book which contains all of them.

The chapters are, for the most part, self-explanatory. But a word needs to be said about three of them. James Barr, who greatly helped our discussions not only by his specialist knowledge of the Old Testament but also by his experience of ecumenical discussions on the authority of Scripture, was not able to attend all our meetings, and was prevented by other commitments from preparing a chapter for this book. But at an earlier stage he had provided us with an informal and somewhat tentative essay, which we prevailed on him to allow us to include in something like its original form. The ideas it contains we felt to be important to our theme, though we acknowledge that he would certainly have wished, had time allowed, to present them in a more finished and systematic form.

Geza Vermes is well known as a Jewish scholar with a keen interest in gospel criticism and in the historical aspects of Christology. We have greatly appreciated the contribution he has made to our discussions from the beginning, and we are glad to be able to include a chapter from his pen. This necessarily presents a point of view very

*Ed. John Hick.

vii

different from that of the rest of us, but we have ourselves learnt a great deal from it, and we believe our readers also will find that it throws a new and helpful light on our theme.

Finally, a word must be said about the Dean of Durham's sermon which concludes our collection. Peter Baelz gave up his Chair at Oxford in January 1980, and was therefore absent for the last year of our discussions. But he continued to follow our progress with keen interest, and had always felt a particular concern that the work of academic theologians should be seen to be both relevant and helpful to those who have the responsibility of communicating the gospel. The sermon he delivered in Durham Cathedral on Christmas Day 1980 was written after prolonged reflection on our common enterprise, and is offered as a tentative example of the way in which one who has ventured on the kind of thinking which is explored in this book may still with integrity preach the fundamental truths of the Christian faith.

A.E.H.

1

Christian Propositions and Christian Stories

ANTHONY HARVEY

In what sense, if at all, may we say that Jesus is divine? For many centuries this has been the central question of Christology; indeed, many would say that it is the central question of Christian theology itself. The impact of the publication of *The Myth of God Incarnate* was perhaps mainly due to the fact that the book addressed itself to a question which lies at the very heart of the Christian faith, and appeared (in view of the most natural, non-technical meaning of the title) to offer a negative answer to it. Its authors were all convinced Christian theologians who had nevertheless come to the conclusion that it is no longer possible to formulate the belief that Christ is divine in a way that is intellectually satisfying, and they consequently set out to show that this belief is not in fact so central to Christianity as has usually been thought, and that its prominence in traditional Christian theology has been due to something like a misunderstanding of the implications of the original Christian revelation.

For the most part, the authors of this present collection of essays, though they recognize the force of this argument, find themselves unable to accept its conclusion. From the fact that it may now be difficult to formulate a doctrine which corresponds to the traditional Christian belief in the divinity of Christ, it does not seem to us to follow that the belief itself must be abandoned. To put it another way: for many centuries Christian theology has been thought to consist in expressing the Christian faith in a series of logically coherent propositions. But in fact it is not only propositions that we call 'true', nor are our beliefs expressed exclusively in doctrine. It may be possible to believe that Jesus was more than human (in the usual sense of that word) even if our contemporary philosophical background provides us with no means of expressing this more-than-human-ness in propositional form. These essays may therefore be understood, not as a refutation of the entire *Myth of God* approach, but as an exploration of the diverse ways in which we in fact express ourselves when we seek to articulate our deepest beliefs. By setting the question of Christology in this wider context, we hope we may succeed in reducing that sense of dismay which was caused by the apparently negative conclusions of *The Myth*.

1

The proposition that Jesus is divine – that he is 'Son of God' in that particular sense which is intended by traditional Christian theology – is one that appears to be an answer to the question of Jesus's nature and status. But why is such a question asked in the first place? It is true that at certain times it has seemed important to situate Jesus securely in some metaphysical hierarchy of being, or to defend the Christian faith from contamination by beliefs which did less than justice to the centrality of Christ in the divine dispensation. But today it seems unlikely that this is the main concern and motivation of those who are anxious to defend the divinity of Christ. At least two other concerns may be suggested which cause the question of Christology to seem important. The first is the need to be able to say something about Jesus which ascribes to him a unique relationship with God and so makes him in principle different from any other human being; the second is the need to say something about God which will assure the believer of God's deep involvement in the created world and of his intensely personal concern for every individual in it, an involvement and a concern which are somehow made manifest in the person of Jesus. If this is so, then the effect of casting doubt upon Christ's divinity will be to cause strains in other parts of the fabric of Christian belief. These strains are apparent, but not always acknowledged, in contemporary christological discussion, and may serve as an introduction to that widening of the discussion that we propose to undertake.

We may take first the question of the 'uniqueness' of Christ. It has always appeared a matter of extreme difficulty to define the nature of Jesus in a way which does justice both to his unique relationship to God (his 'divinity') and to his humanity. The Chalcedonian definition* appeared to secure an intellectually satisfying balance, but this presupposed the existence of a philosophical context in which the definition could be set. John Hick's apparently naive statement[1] that the Chalcedonian definition is 'meaningless' is presumably intended to draw attention to the fact that it has meaning only if a number of presuppositions are granted of a metaphysical kind with regard to the nature of reality and the component parts of a human being. That is to say, the statement that the Son is of one substance with the Father can no longer be advanced as a proposition which will stand on its own. We have now to say: if it were the case that a distinction could

---

*In A.D. 451 the Council of Chalcedon declared that Jesus Christ, truly God and truly man, was the only-begotten Son of the Father, Word of God, born of the Virgin Mary, in whose single person the two natures (human and divine) were neither confused nor separated. In saying this it claimed to be building upon what had been said at earlier councils, and particularly at the Council of Nicea, which had declared that God the Son, Jesus Christ the Word, was of the same substance as the Father; that is to say, his divinity was in no sense inferior, and what could be said of the Father must equally be said of the Son.

meaningfully be made between substance and essence when speaking both of God and of a man, then the divinity of Jesus could be expressed in terms of identity of substance. To put the matter more simply, we should no longer say 'The Son is of one substance with the Father', but rather, 'It is as if the Son were of one substance with the Father' (where 'as if' is a way of recognizing that a set of assumptions are being made which may not be true other than in an analogical sense). Indeed, it is arguable that this is precisely what the authors of the Chalcedonian definition intended, and that it was the exigencies of subsequent dogma which erected it into an expression of ultimate truth.

Nevertheless, this concentration on defining the relationship of Jesus with God in metaphysical terms inevitably resulted in a neglect of those features of his personality which made him in any way exceptional among human beings. The concern was more to discover what could be said about Jesus's 'divinity' without actually making him other than human, than to incorporate any of his specifically human features in the definition of his nature. His humanity became little more than a theoretical datum, necessary for the sake of theological truth, but unrelated to the human characteristics borne by the Jesus who had actually existed. It was in reaction to this that a concern for Jesus's specific humanity began to appear, first in the 'kenosis' theory of the nineteenth century, and then in the profoundly human-centred Christology of recent years, of which J. A. T. Robinson's *The Human Face of God* is a good example. The recent fundamental questioning of the christological tradition is no more than a continuation of this trend. Its authors rightly observe that it calls into question all language which appears to ascribe 'divinity' to Jesus; but they have been less quick to notice that it also makes it difficult to give any account of the uniqueness of Jesus. Phrases such as 'decisive act of God in Jesus', or 'focus of redemptive history' are still widely used; but if the attempt is abandoned to define the special relationship which may be held to exist between Jesus and God, there seem to remain no grounds on which it may be argued that Jesus was in principle different from other men, nor (in consequence) that the Christian religion has a claim to truth greater than any other. Indeed, the strain which this places on Christian theology is particularly apparent in discussions of the relationship of Christianity to other religions.

The relationship of God to creation is an equally important element in the concern to define the relationship of Jesus with God. One of the central messages of the incarnation is felt to be God's total self-involvement in the frailty and the suffering of mankind. 'God was in Christ, reconciling all men to himself' provides almost the key text for this aspect of Christology. But again, great difficulties arise when this concern has to be reconciled with a 'high' view of the relationship between Jesus and God. If God was truly present in Jesus, how could Jesus suffer without God also suffering – an implication which again could be coped with only with the aid of a highly sophisticated set of metaphysical distinctions.

A possible way out of this difficulty has been explored recently by (among others) G. W. H. Lampe.[2] Attention is drawn to the way in which the Bible expresses man's faith in the involvement of God in human affairs, namely by means of the Holy Spirit. Here it is evident that biblical man saw the matter differently from modern man. Today, the evidence for God's involvement in the world is usually found in such things as answers to prayer, miraculous healing, or the growth in power and sanctity of a Christian church, community, or group. But in the Bible it is God's Spirit which intervenes in human affairs, which manifests his power and which (through the prophets) makes plain his will, his demands, and his unmerited grace. Why should one not say, then, that the incarnation was the greatest and most decisive of all these manifestations of God's Spirit; and that the constancy of God's love for the world and involvement in it is shown precisely in that although Jesus, like the prophets before him, was rejected, and although this rejection, taking the form of crucifixion, was apparently a total and final expression of man's response to the Spirit of God, yet the continuing operation of that same Spirit in the Church shows the inexhaustible nature of God's gracious concern for men, and the constant and indestructible availability of our redemption?

One of the weaknesses of this approach is that, though it may give a satisfactory account of the crucifixion, it can attach little significance to the resurrection.[3] But there is another implication which should be noticed. The Spirit of God is by its nature not restricted to one type of manifestation. It continues to work within the Church and also outside the Church. It was at work in Old Testament times and it is at work in the vastly different circumstances of today. It follows that, however much the life and death of Jesus may seem to have been a turning point in the history of the world (or at least of our civilization), it is exceedingly difficult to find reasons why it should be regarded as the 'decisive' or 'focal' moment in the relationship between God and man. Why should not the Spirit be equally active in other great world religions or in other periods of world history? As with human-centred Christology, so with Spirit-centred Christology, it seems impossible to justify the conviction that Jesus was in any sense unique.

If, then, the question of Christology is a considerably wider one than it seemed at first sight, then it is reasonable to suppose that the means of answering it may be more varied and complex than are allowed for in traditional theology. To describe the unique significance of a person or event, one does not necessarily resort to a series of logically coherent propositions. One may write a love-song or a novel, one may create a work of art or tell a story; and of all these it makes sense (as we shall see)[4] to say that they are either true or false, whether or not the truth they contain can be reduced to a series of logically acceptable propositions. The primary source of our knowledge about Jesus is not in any case a doctrinal treatise, but is essentially *narrative*. Might it not be, therefore, that a more appropriate way of expressing Jesus's relationship with God and God's relationship with men is that which is most characteristic of the Bible: that of telling a story? There is, after all, good precedent for such an approach, in that Jesus himself, along with most oriental religious teachers, used stories in order to give teaching about God, and indeed New Testament statements in general about the place of Jesus in the divine economy tend to have a narrative form (God was in Christ, the Holy Spirit has been poured, etc.). Could it be, then, that narrative theology, rather than propositional theology, offers a solution to the difficulty of expressing the uniqueness of Christ? Might it be possible to tell a story about Jesus which is different in principle from that about any other person, and which expresses more satisfactorily than any dogmatic proposition the relationship of God with his creation?

A theologian might well offer immediate resistance to such a proposal. If theological truth is to be expressed in the form of stories, what room is left for any theological discipline? Must we now hand over all responsibility to literary critics, who will alone be able to tell us which story or stories deserve to be treated as classic or normative? But this reaction would be too hasty. A moment's reflection shows that discrimination between one kind of story and another remains a vital theological enterprise. The so-called gnostic heresies of the second and third centuries, for example, may be described as a preoccupation with the wrong kind of story. The chief personage in the story became a divine or semi-divine being, who 'came down' for a period and assumed human form; but the human or historical side of the story was secondary, all the emphasis being placed on the aspect which may properly be called 'mythical', that is, the representation of some alleged truth about God by means of a story which is 'always true', and which has no necessary reference to any particular time or place. The response of the Church was to stress the fact that the story of Jesus was a story about a real person who lived at a particular time and a particular place, and about whom a great many particular facts were known by means of an unbroken and reliable chain of witnesses. As Ignatius of Antioch put it in the early stages of the controversy, Jesus 'was really crucified and really died'.[5] Then, as now, the discrimination between one kind of story and another was an authentic and necessary task for the theologian.

5

Indeed, we can give a certain precision to this task. We can distinguish, for example, between three senses in which the story of Jesus may be said to be 'true':

1. It may be true as a record of historical events. Here we must be careful not to impose criteria which would be inappropriate to other records of events which have come down to us from the ancient world. Every historian selects and interprets the facts to some extent, and we have no right to expect that the facts about Jesus should be accessible in an exceptionally pure and uninterpreted form: as with all historical records, we must expect to have to allow for a certain interpretative bias, without, for that reason, concluding that the story of Jesus is not 'true'. Moreover, we need not demand that every detail should be historically correct. Legendary features readily attach themselves to the recollections of great men: circumstantial details are forgotten or confused; gaps in the tradition are ignored or padded out; matters which may seem important to later generations are passed over in silence. But these imperfections, which will be present in the records of any personage of ancient history, do not prevent us from forming a judgement whether we have a narrative which is true in basic essentials and broad outline. If, for example, we were to accept S. G. F. Brandon's thesis[6] that the gospels are totally tendentious, and that Jesus was in reality a violent revolutionary, we would judge that the gospel story is not true. But this is not the impression which the Gospels have made on the vast majority of their readers, whether Christian or non-Christian. Whatever may be the case with a large number of details, and however much Christian interpretation may have been added to the original facts, in broad outline the story of Jesus as recorded in the Gospels commends itself, both to literary critics and to New Testament scholars, as substantially true.

2. A story may be true, not only to historical fact, but in the further sense of 'true to life', 'true to experience'. Stories are told, and hold the attention, for a variety of reasons: they may be fantastic or realistic; based on fact or imagination; rapid and sensational or slow and impressionistic. But the stories which are great, which live and are treasured, are ones which represent aspects of human life and experience which are sensed to be true. If we say that *War and Peace* is 'true to life', we do not mean primarily that the descriptions of the Napoleonic Wars are historically correct, but that the characters are credible and their actions and responses offer a glimpse of human nature as it is. Applied to the gospel narratives, this type of truth offers a further criterion. If the story of Jesus represented him as some kind of freak, acting and speaking irrationally or incoherently, the story would have no truth other than in its approximation to historical fact. If, on the other hand, the story of Jesus is such that it awakens a response in the reader by moving him, challenging him, and enligh-

tening him, we may say that it is true also in the way that other great stories may be true – true to life, true to experience.

3. Stories need not, and usually do not, consist entirely of action. They contain also discourse and reflection. These constituents may also invite judgement on whether they are true. The explicit teaching given by the hero of the story may be true or false, acceptable or inacceptable; and in particular the hope or vision for the future which is explicitly or implicitly offered in the course of the story will be an important element in securing a place for it in the memory and imagination of subsequent generations. Thucydides wrote his history, not as the record of a unique and unrepeatable event, but in the belief that the trends and causes which he identified would be true of all future conflicts, so that his story would serve as a warning and an example. A story may be true in both the senses so far defined but be seen to have relevance only to the specific circumstances of its own time. But if a story also offers a vision for the future which is such as to inspire the devotion and effort of subsequent generations, we may say that it is true in this sense also – true to the future, giving the truth about man's destiny, and so forth.

There is, then, an important task for theology which consists in the monitoring and control of the Christian story. It must ensure that each telling of the story satisfies all the appropriate truth-conditions. In particular, this approach to theology may offer a solution to the problem from which we started, namely that of the uniqueness of Jesus Christ and the propriety of speaking of him as in some way the decisive manifestation of God's involvement in the lives of men. One may compare the truth of the Christian story with that of the stories of the other world religions. This matter of the relationship of Christianity to other religions has only recently come to be seen as a fundamental question of theology – the arrangement of Hans Küng's *On Being a Christian* is a fair example of what is now seen to be a theological priority, namely the justification for setting forth the apparently final and exclusive claims of the Christian religion in a social context in which only a minority accept the claims of any revealed religion, and of that minority a large number of people are adherents of other faiths. In the terms of traditional (that is, propositional) theology, this task has seemed to present an inescapable dilemma. Either (it seems) it is necessary to say firmly that the Christian revelation is true, and that other religions are therefore false except in so far as they may include certain doctrines of God which approximate to Christian teaching – a judgement which is now widely felt to do less than justice to the achievements of other faiths; or else one must go to the other extreme and grant that God may equally have revealed himself in other religions, and that Christianity possesses no more than a kind of specific cultural claim upon the allegiance of those whose background has particularly prepared them for it – a position which would not be repudiated by a number of Christian theologians today, though it seems (a point well made by Stephen Neill in *The Truth of God Incarnate*)[7] to do scant justice to the convictions and experience of contemporary Christian missionaries and of those who are persecuted for their faith.

The theologian who is concerned with the truth of the Christian story (in the senses outlined above) rather than of Christian propositions may be able to offer a way out of this dilemma. He may study the 'story' told by other great religions, and judge that in each case that story may be true in certain senses. He may grant, for instance, that the story told by Islam is true in the first of our suggested senses (that of its historical truth) but defective in certain other senses (such as that it is not true to the experience of a society which assigns equal importance to women as to men, and that its vision of the future has not the comprehensiveness necessary for a truly universal religion); or he may judge that Buddhism has a story which is barely true in the first (historical) sense but has a great measure of truth in its interpretation of the relationship of man to the rest of creation – and so forth. And so, without having to deny the truth (in these various senses) of other great religions, he may be able to make out a reasonable case for the claim that the Christian story is true in a way that no other religion is – true in all the possible and significant ways in which a story can be true.[8]

However, the argument so far has been somewhat misleading, in that it has appeared to assume that the content of the Christian story is nothing other than the story of Jesus. This assumption has doubtless been an inevitable result of the concentration of previous generations of theologians on the person of Christ as the unique topic of Christology. But if one is now to move from 'propositional' to 'narrative' theology, one must not assume that the centre of interest will remain, as it was before, the person of Jesus himself, and that the 'story' we are concerned with will be simply the story of Jesus. As soon as Christian theology is set in the context of its relationship with other faiths, it is clear that the comparison cannot be simply between Christ and Mohammed, or Christ and the Buddha, but between the entire story of the Christian movement and the entire story of Islam or Buddhism. Indeed, the whole context of this narrative approach is necessarily different from that of traditional doctrinal propositions. In seeking to define the nature and person of Christ it was both possible and proper to concentrate upon him alone and to seek to define the relationship of that one person to God and to man. But as soon as one tries to tell the story of Jesus, it becomes plain that this cannot be done adequately without giving an account both of the circumstances which prepared for his coming and of the subsequent unfolding of the movement which followed his life and death.[9]

It follows that the content of the story cannot be merely the things concerning Jesus. The story, that is to say, cannot be identical with Scripture. This is one aspect of the error and limitation of fundamentalism. In his reply to *The Myth of God Incarnate* Michael Green [10] evidently felt that it was sufficient to tell the biblical story over and over again: its superiority to any rival story would become apparent, and this would show that Christians who were attempting to tell the story in a radically different way must be in error. But Scripture, though it may be (as we shall see) a determinative part of the story, cannot be the whole of it. The story includes the response of Christians down the centuries to the telling of the original story, and the differing forms in which the story has been retold in order to be comprehensible to different ages and cultures are themselves part of the story. But this consideration opens up a further task for theology: that of distinguishing between one retelling of the story and another, and of judging which of these may properly be included in the total Christian story.

This task is of course only a new form of a traditional one. In the past it amounted to the definition of orthodox doctrine. In order to judge whether an opinion was acceptable within the Church or was heretical, the criterion applied was an existing system of doctrinal statements: if the new opinion was incompatible with this, it must be pronounced heretical. Admittedly, the churches of the Reformation have introduced a good deal of variety and complexity into this simple procedure. As S.W. Sykes has shown in his recent book on Anglicanism,[11] the criterion by which an opinion may be judged Anglican or heretical is one which may be formed from sources as various as the 1662 Prayer Book and the writings of William Temple. But even when it is granted that the task may now be extremely difficult, it is still assumed that its accomplishment must be possible in the form of certain doctrinal propositions.

If we now call this assumption into question, the criterion which is needed is that which will decide between the truth of different stories. To be more precise, we have to decide which retellings of the Christian story (in the somewhat larger sense given above) can legitimately find a place in the total 'story' of the Christian movement as it continues to live in our own days. And it is difficult to see how there can be any criterion other than that which consists in, or is implied by the existence of, Scripture itself. This is indeed empirically demonstrated by the reaction of ordinary practising Christians to *The Myth of God Incarnate* – even if it was a reaction mainly to the title. It was felt instinctively that such an approach is incompatible, not necessarily with a particular proposition in the Christian tradition, but with what the Bible is about in general. The Bible tells a story, and the story it tells is plainly not a 'myth' in the usual sense of that word. Therefore

9

to suggest that the Christian story can now be retold as a 'myth' is felt to be an illegitimate enterprise for a Christian to undertake.

How does this criterion work? Some conservative theologians would regard this as quite simple. The Christian story is one that can be and must be told over and over again, and there is no need for any substantial retelling: Scripture itself is sufficient. But our whole problem arises out of something which seems to have been characteristic of the story of the Christian movement right from the beginning, namely the felt necessity constantly to retell the story in a way which will convey its meaning in every different period and every different culture; and a criterion which imposes scriptural content and scriptural form is clearly too narrow to embrace the rich variety of retellings which have in fact gained a legitimate place within the Christian tradition. Nevertheless, it is clear that Scripture does exercise a certain control, and by way of illustration three ways can be suggested (which are not necessarily either normative or exhaustive, but which seem normally to be operative) in which it does so.

1. Any retelling must recognize that Scripture exists and is irreplaceable. One way (and it is arguable that it is now the only way) in which membership of a church, or of the Church, may be defined is by the acceptance of the continuing authority of Scripture. A Christian individual or group which has begun regularly to read some literature other than, and instead of, the Bible at its worship (however edifying and 'Christian' that literature may be) is beginning to lose its solidarity with the Church. Similarly, a church which has come to accept another writing as at least as authoritative as the Bible (for example, Mormons or Christian Scientists) will cease to be part of the Church. This means that any retelling of the story within the Church will be one which is recognizably a retelling of the story of which Scripture is the first and most authoritative record. The doctrine of the Assumption, for instance, causes difficulty to a great many Christians because it appears to tell a story which is not present in Scripture even *in nuce*. Contemporary preaching of the gospel, on the other hand, is felt to be within the Christian tradition, however unconventional its style, so long as it is genuinely concerned to present the gist of the story which is in the Bible and not some other story.

2. The retelling must share the overriding concern of the New Testament to give unique importance to Jesus. As we have seen, this means that the story which is told about Jesus must be one which, in some respects at least, could not be told about any other person. Precisely what the respects are in which this is so is a question which may receive different answers. In certain periods Jesus has seemed uniquely powerful, or uniquely good, or uniquely related to the purposes of God for the world. A retelling of the story which explored any of these aspects might legitimately take its place in the Christian

tradition. But one which (for example) represented Jesus as only one of a possible succession of *hasidim*, or the Christian movement as only one of the currents which have gone to make up man's religious understanding, would not be acceptable as a retelling which lay within the progress of the continuing Christian 'story'.

3. The retelling must be 'scriptural' in the further sense that it affirms and illustrates the involvement of God in his creation. The story of Jesus has been frequently retold in recent years, either with no explicit reference to God (as in the pop theatre), or in a deliberately atheistic context (as by certain Marxist writers). These retellings, though they may incidentally serve the Christian cause by drawing attention to Jesus, nevertheless cannot be regarded as legitimate versions of the Christian story. The biblical narrative throughout makes God the protagonist of every story, and portrays Jesus as the expression of God's love for the world. Whatever idiom is used in a contemporary retelling, the fully Christian character of the story can be preserved only if it gives due place to the interaction between God and his creation.

In conclusion, two general comments may be made on the argument as presented above.

First, it could be said that it is transparently circular. We have said that it is not sufficient to retell the story again and again simply as it stands in Scripture: each generation, each culture, must retell it in its own way. Yet we have also said that there is no criterion for distinguishing between a Christian and a non-Christian retelling other than is provided by Scripture itself. But (it may be said) it is precisely this alleged sufficiency and authority of Scripture which is at issue. It can be argued that the priorities and emphases of the scriptural story, as well as its cultural and intellectual context, are meaningless to the modern mind; and that therefore the story must now be told in a way so radically different from the scriptural way that Scripture itself cannot provide a basis for judgement.

To which it must be replied that every presentation of the Christian religion is in some sense a circular argument. It must be consistent with itself and compatible with all known facts about the world and about human experience, but it will remain a closed or circular system: it cannot be checked against some external standard of religious truth. Similarly, the Christian story is one of which each retelling must be in some way consistent with the original, and to deny the normative character of the original is to seek to stand outside the system and to introduce some independent criterion. This is of course sometimes done. It could be said, for instance, that existentialist theologians have found an objective norm in a kind of authentic experience, on the basis of which the judgement can be made that the Paul of Romans is an authoritative expositor of the Christian faith while the author of the Pastorals represents (in Bultmann's phrase) only a 'bourgeois adaptation' of it. But the main stream of Christian theology has always recognized that it works within a closed system.

But there is a further point which is more relevant to our argument. The authority of Scripture is not an independent and isolated factor. It cannot be explained without reference to the fact that the Christian movement in its various manifestations has always ascribed authority to it. This is not by any means to deny that Scripture may be 'inspired'. Indeed, Scripture undoubtedly represents for a Christian one of the means by which God has been active in the world, and a channel by which he still addresses an individual. But it does mean that the notion of the authority of Scripture can be understood completely only when there is reference to the use made of it by the Christian community. To speak of 'authority' outside this specific context is to fall into the error of those who, in the nineteenth century, assumed that because the Bible is authoritative in matters of religion it must be authoritative also in matters of cosmogony and biology. But the community of cosmogonists or biologists does not accept the authority of the Bible in its own field, and there is no reason why it should do so; nor do even Christians necessarily accept it as an authority for ancient chronology. The kind of authority it bears for them can be discovered only by studying the ways in which their belief and practice are actually affected by it.

The ways in which this control is exercised has varied and still does vary considerably. When we are seeking to make a judgement on a particular retelling of the Christian story, we cannot ask whether it is 'scriptural' merely in the abstract; we have to ask whether the kind of control exerted over it by Scripture is actually represented by the exegetical or expository practice of any group of Christians whom we recognize (or would be prepared to recognize) thereby as part of the Church. That is to say, the argument may be circular, but the circle includes more than just Scripture and its retelling: it embraces the entire history and present extent of the Church, the whole 'phenomenon of Christianity'. To judge whether a story is Christian involves a judgement on whether the group or person who is telling it can be regarded as part of the Church.

The second comment is simply the admission that the concept of 'story', and of 'narrative theology', is necessarily imprecise, and may even turn out to be no more than a theological fashion. But its function in our argument is not necessarily to replace what we have called propositional theology, but to show that propositions may not be the only respectable means of expressing theological truth. The essence of the *Myth* approach has been to call into question even the possibility of expressing certain fundamental Christian doctrines in a form which is acceptable today. So long as the only means of formulating Christian truth is thought to be in terms of propositional doctrine, this may indeed be .correct. But as soon as it is granted that there may be another way of doing theology, or indeed a number of ways, then it ceases to be necessary to assume that certain aspects of the Christian faith, which have traditionally been regarded as fundamental, can no longer be accepted simply because the propositions in which they are expressed seem to have lost their meaning. In particular, the unique relationship between Jesus and God, and the continuing involvement of God in the destiny of men, are Christian convictions which will not readily be shaken and which will not be denied expression merely because they can no longer be formulated in a set of logically related propositions.

NOTES

1. *The Myth of God Incarnate*, ed. John Hick (1977), p. 178.
2. *God as Spirit* (1977).
3. Cf. G. W. H. Lampe, op. cit., p. 158: 'This experience of participation in Christ's sonship . . . does not seem in any way to depend on whether a resurrection-event actually happened.'
4. See below, Chapter 3.
5. *Trallians* 9.
6. S.G.F. Brandon, *Jesus and the Zealots* (1967).
7. Ed. M. Green (1977), pp. 84–6.
8. Ninian Smart, in *Truth and Dialogue* (ed. John Hick, 1974), p. 45, points out that little attention has been paid to the meanings and criteria of 'truth' in the comparative study of religion.
9. Some recognition of this need to enlarge the area of christological study may account for the popularity of the expression 'the Christ-event', which is discussed in Chapter 7.
10. *The Truth of God Incarnate*, *passim*.
11. *The Integrity of Anglicanism* (1978), *passim*.

2

Some Thoughts on Narrative, Myth and Incarnation

JAMES BARR

IT is a common observation that narrative is one major literary form of the Bible, and we would not go far wrong if we said that most people consider it to be the main literary form of the Bible. Narrative can be defined ostensively: Genesis consists of narrative, so do the Books of Samuel and Kings, and so also do the Gospels. There are of course other literary genres in the Bible, and from some points of view some of these might compete with narrative for centrality: such are, perhaps, the Hebrew poetry of the Psalms, the oracular utterances of the prophets, and the epistolary matter of the New Testament letters. But, however great the importance of these other types, it remains true that in modern times very great attention has been directed upon the narrative material. It has been the existence of this large body of narrative material that has been taken to justify, in part at least, the claim that Judaism and Christianity are historical religions. Similarly, it is the existence of this material that has been used as the basis for the claim that the mental co-ordinates of biblical man were formed for him by an essentially historical body of data. The term *history*, however, is noticeably and intentionally absent from the title of this present paper. That the material is narrative seems to be beyond question and this may be taken as a neutral and objective term. If we go a step farther and say that the material is *story* we may be using a value term but it is one which we shall defend as useful on the basis of explorations to follow. One reason why we say *story* rather than *history* can be made clear at the beginning: history may not succeed in giving a true and accurate account of events that took place, but at least it must be supposed to have sought to give such an account or to have presupposed the possibility of such an account; story on the other hand may not so intend. Nevertheless, biblical story has considerable contact with history, in the sense of events that in some form really took place. Biblical story is not a simple reportage of history, but it is also not a fictional story having no contact with history. Thus I consider its relation to history to be a tangential one, or better, that of a spiral which runs back and forward across history, sometimes touching it or coinciding with it. Just how close it is to history, or just how far from it, is an interesting question: one that we should accept

14

will never be solved, and one such that theology will never be in a position to legislate over how close or how remote the relation may be. In other words, theology, and faith with it, have just to accept the variability of this relation and its uncertainty.[1]

Now a main characteristic of the major biblical story is that it is a sort of foundation story. It begins from some crucial datum point and runs down to some other point, the closing point being often only vaguely designated. In the Old Testament the story begins with the creation of the world and runs down to some later crucial point: with the Samaritans the entry into Canaan, with the Jews the Babylonian exile or, to be more exact, the lifting up of the head of Jehoiachin ex-king of Judah by Amel-Marduk in the thirty-seventh year of his exile. Thereafter we have some memoirs like those of Nehemiah and Ezra but these are only loosely attached to the main story, and the same is true of Esther and other such pieces. The story leads up to some decisive point and thereafter – and this is one of the differences from an interpretation of *history* – it stops and is allowed to fall into the past. In the New Testament, similarly, the Gospels begin with the arrival of Jesus, whether his birth or his meeting with John the Baptist, and the story runs down to the resurrection and/or ascension; Luke goes on to the arrival of St Paul in Rome. The completion of the basic story can be, and is, followed by a period in which there is little sign of historical interest or indeed of narrative creativity. No one wrote a history of Jewish life under the Persians, apart from the limited memoirs of Ezra and Nehemiah, although this period was of vital importance for the Jews and indeed for the formation of the Old Testament itself, and little historical writing was done by Christians about the time from St Paul's arrival in Rome until a long time afterwards. On the other hand, even as a foundation story the story is a sequential and cumulative one, and in this respect is unlike stories like that of Job, which could be set in any time, or parables which might be true of any time, or anecdotes such as we find in the rabbinic literature that are connected with a particular person as storyteller but have no particular connection with some slot or position in a larger story.

Now this brings us to an important aspect of biblical story. Such story is by its nature set in the past but this does not necessarily mean that the past is its only, or even its main, purport. Here again we mark the difference from history. Of much biblical narrative it may perhaps be said that although its setting is in the past its purport lies in the present and future. The motivation of much Israelite storytelling was not to discover or to relate how things had been long ago but to provide accounts of things as they now are or to provide paradigms for future hope. Conversely, predictive statements about the future are not there just for their future reference, but also for their paradigmatic quality in the present and the sense they make of the recorded past by telling the reader where, ultimately, this past is going.[2] A story like that of Abraham was told not because the writer wanted to communicate how things had been back in the second millennium B.C. but – or at least but also – because he wanted to provide a paradigm for hope for a promise that was yet to come. If, however, this was his purpose it was not basically essential that the elements of his story should be historically accurate. Indeed, the more future-directed a story was in its actual aim and purport the more irrelevant and indeed impossible it became for it to be historically correct.

Our vision is clouded here, I suggest, by our inherited doctrines of revelation – inherited not from ancient times but from more recent theological developments – which have tended to specify revelation through past events. And I do not wish to diminish the importance of past events in revelation. The fact remains that too exclusive an emphasis upon them can cause us much trouble in coping with the question now before us, that is, the analysis and evaluation of our main written story, the narrative core of Old and New Testaments. Perhaps we can put it in this way: we have often talked of Scripture as a 'record' and used the conceptual pair 'record and revelation', but I am suggesting that Scripture is not a record at all or at any rate is not primarily a record. It is a story furnishing a basic understanding that will give substance for present faith and future hope. If Christianity is a historical religion, it is equally true to say that it is an eschatological religion, and equally important.

Let us consider further how this applies to the Gospels. Some elements in the Gospel story, or some versions or strands, may be not so much a historical record of what Jesus said and did, but rather the earliest Church's interpreted expression of him, given to following generations as a paradigm for living communion with him and future hope in him. To categorize the level of their purport as 'history' seems to me to be mistaken. I cannot agree that the words of John 21.24 are evidence that the authenticity of that entire Gospel, or of all the Gospels, consisted in their *historical* character. Whatever we make of this verse, John taken as a whole seems to be good evidence of the contrary. The character and the mystery of the Fourth Gospel is in no small measure created by the peculiar mixture within it of on the one hand precise historical detail and on the other deeply doctrinal meditation of a kind that is most unlikely to have been so expressed at the time; and this charm and tension is lost if we universalize either of these aspects.[3] The idiosyncratic style of Jesus's speech in the Synoptic Gospels, which does much to present him as a real and complete character, is in considerable measure dispersed in the Jesus of John, whose diction in many discourses has the same general style as that of the Johannine letters. And take an incident like the expulsion of the money-changers from the Temple. In the Synoptics this comes at the beginning of Passion Week, but in John at a quite different stage, early in the tale of the ministry. How can such a discrepancy be laid at the doors of writers, the quality of whose work is to be directly linked to its authenticity as *history*? Writing of this incident, Anthony Harvey says:[4]

> If we wish to know in what order things actually happened, we have to make our choice between the two versions, and allow for the fact that one or the other (or both) may have been deliberately rearranged in order to bring out better the significance of each period of Jesus's life.

Those who would 'deliberately rearrange' the sequence of major events in the story must have been people who were, at least at certain places, rather free in their dependence on historical fact. Conversely, the more we insist on connecting the authority of the Gospels with their authenticity as *history*, the more we shall have to fear that their authority will be damaged by the fact of the discrepancies between them.[5]

In other words, the narratives of the Gospels, as we have them, may have been generated by the desire to narrate history, but may also have been generated by the desire to express significance. I would not like to try to disentangle the elements of each and, from the point of view of Christian believing, do not think it to be of immediate and direct importance, although there is also a task of critical historical reconstruction which must also ultimately have a bearing upon belief. The story may well be full of historical elements, but this does not mean that all of it is history, indeed the text itself suggests that it is not. Some of it may have been substantially rewritten, to use a new diction, to express significance in a clearer way, and to incorporate elements and perspectives which in earlier versions were not there. This was no novelty in biblical narrative: Chronicles was a rewrite of Samuel–Kings, and Jubilees a rewrite of Genesis. John, and indeed all the Gospels, may perhaps be similarly viewed. If it is true that items were 'deliberately' rearranged so as to bring out significance, this means that the rewriters were actually aware that they were altering the previously understood historical sequence and creating a picture that was in this respect contrary to fact, and believed that this was legitimate for the expression of theological significance. Of course all history has the task of explaining significance, but what was done with the expulsion of the money-changers was not that an *explanation* of significance was provided, but that the placing of the events was altered. In other words, in my terms, history was modified for the sake of a better story. The plethora of historical detail and circumstantiality in biblical narrative does not alter this. The purport of the stories was not coincident with history: they were above all *authorita-tive* statements for future generations, authoritative statements of how one should see how it had been.[6]

One might without irreverence consider the analogy of the histori-cal novel: let us think of Tolstoy's *War and Peace*. The historical novel has to have a historical setting and stand within a certain recognizable unity provided by that setting, in this case Russia at the time of the Napoleonic Wars. People must speak and dress and act in ways that remind of that time and place. Circumstantial details will be welcome. Gross anachronisms will be avoided, and gross historical dispropor-tions will also be eschewed: for example, it would be unlikely that such a novel would tell a story in which Napoleon retreated straight from Smolensk and never reached Moscow at all. But within these wider limits things can be different: persons may be fictional, though they must be plausible as persons of that time, battles may be fought where no battle really took place, and the order of events may be altered. History and a measure of historical verisimilitude are a neces-sity for such a writing; but it does not really purport to be history. In many respects its purport is something more like the world-view of the author. Yet on the other side it tells the historical story well enough: if it were the only written document of the time we had, we would have in it a good general historical source. Of course, the analogy is not a very good one – the aspect of *authority*, all-important for the Gospels, lies entirely outside its range; but it brings out aspects which are quite relevant for biblical narrative.[7]

If we may look at things in this way, it leads us to the question: what sort of contact does all this have with the use of *myth* as applied to the incarnation or to other similar central features of Christian belief? For instance, the idea of the biblical story as a foundation story might make contact with accepted ideas of myth, for many myths are located in the beginning of things, they are supposed to tell how the basic order of the universe was laid down. Would it be right to say that the biblical narrative is in this sense a 'myth'?

I take it that we can ignore for present purposes the crude notion that the term *myth* implies no more than untruth, deceit, unreality, falsehood: the existence of this notion is a practical difficulty in the use of the word *myth*, but it makes no difference to the discussion of the realities meant. In biblical studies, however, quite apart from this crude notion, the fact remains that majority opinion – at least in the last decades – has been opposed to any general application of the term *myth* to biblical narrative. At least in Old Testament studies (where the Bultmannian ideas of demythologization and the like were never very influential) the classic argument has been as follows. History and myth are diametrically opposed entities. The Old Testament is basi-cally a historical work, at least in its main narrative sections.

Remnants of myth may be discerned all over the place, but this myth has been separated from its original basis and on reintegration into Israelite historical narrative it has come to be historicized. From this point of view the Old Testament, far from being myth, is a most potent demythologizing force. This argument, however, may now have to be somewhat modified if the opinion I have expressed is right and if the Old Testament material is not as clearly historical in character as had been supposed.

The opinion just cited has often been associated with a further view, namely that myth deals essentially with eternal verities. It is static and depicts something that, having been established in the beginning in the world of the gods, or in the common world of gods and men, will then simply continue for ever. It is thus a guarantee of a permanent conservative view of the world. In so far as any movement takes place in myth, according to this view, it is a cyclic movement, like the growth and withering of the vegetation, the cycle of death and rebirth. Ancient Canaanite mythology was a sort of literary depiction of the world of sex and fertility: it linked up precisely with the abuses of fertility cults, Baalism, cultic prostitution, and the like, which the Hebrew prophets attacked, and it similarly gave guarantees to the world of social injustice which they also attacked. From this point of view the abolition of myth was an essential service furnished by the Old Testament and thereby was also the means of operation of its dynamic of social criticism.

It is not so certain now that this line of argument can be maintained. If the biblical story can be thought of as a sort of foundation story, then it too could conceivably operate to establish something that will last for ever, and at least some strata of the biblical literature may have intended exactly this. Certain strata emphasize the establishment of a polity and a legal/ritual complex, and are correspondingly lacking in suggestions that such a polity and complex might come to be rejected by God himself – a suggestion that other strata, notably in the prophets, are quite ready to make. Another difficulty lies in the fact that, in spite of much increased knowledge of Canaanite religion from its own texts, the links between its myths and the abuses denounced by the Israelite prophets still remain rather obscure. Moreover, some of the social ideas which animate Israelite society and are approved by law and prophets alike – for instance, the image of the king who protects the widow and the orphan – seem to be shared by Israel with those same polytheistic and mythological societies which, according to this model, should not have had these ideals.

More might perhaps be made of the idea that myth is *Götter-geschichte*, that is, that myth takes place essentially in the world of the gods, while the main body of the biblical story takes place in the world of men. Perhaps this is a main service of the monolatrous Israelite tradition with its one transcendent God: because there are no other gods of any significance about, one has no more room for theogonies and such activities as the subject matter for story. In Genesis, the earlier stories, set in a world where things are larger than life, quickly dovetail into the story of human life: life indeed in a world where there is God, where one talks with him and he acts upon one, but nevertheless the basic dimensions of space and time for the story are those provided by human life. Perhaps this feature is even more marked in the Gospels, where to a particularly high degree the action of God is muted and hidden except for his shining through the person and deeds of Jesus. In this sense, if we understand myth as story set in the world of the gods, it might be very important to say that the biblical story, and the gospel story in particular, is not myth.

The trouble with this is that one may have defined myth in a way that will suit one's own case: for it is hard to be sure that all myth does take place within the world of the gods; and, even if it is highly important that the Bible eschews the kind of myth that takes place in that world, it may remain that it retains many other kinds of myth. Scholars talking about myth seem to use a much wider definition of it. For instance, the list of common themes in Greek (mainly heroic) myths provided by Kirk[8] includes a good number that (a) do not take place purely in the world of the gods, and (b) are quite well known in the Bible. For example, no. 14: Deceitful wife, vainly in love with young man, accuses him of rape: it is hardly necessary to cite Potiphar's wife. Again, no. 10: Killing, or attempting to kill, one's own child, perhaps to appease a deity, and often in accordance with an oracle or prophecy: what else do we have in the case of Jephthah's daughter? If these count as myth, and they clearly do in Kirk's language, then the Bible contains a good deal of quite similar myth.

Let us now introduce a further point, which goes back particularly to the idea that myths, or at least Near Eastern myths, are depictions of physical processes or social states. This is what one might call a referential interpretation of myth, and I suggest that the scholarly tradition has been wrong in seeking to provide such an interpretation. It has suggested that a given myth has this form because it represents such and such a real process, observable in nature or in society: for instance, it represents the fertility of the vegetation, or it represents and thereby guarantees the continuation of the society in its existing form. Now I don't think that this is true. Certainly here and there one can find in myths elements which fit very well with fertility or with some other known natural process or social state. But this does not and cannot explain the material of myth as a whole. In fact it explains only small elements, and these are selected and highlighted precisely because under this approach they are meaningful; but it remains that they are only small elements. It may be that many myths have grown

20

from a particular referent or subject in nature or society, in the sense that that entity has given birth to the myth; but once the myth has got going, it has a life of its own. Myths do not represent something in the outside world, or at least they do not have to do so; they feed on themselves, they expand in any direction they like. This means, for our purpose, that it is difficult to think of biblical religion, as people have at times done, as establishing a truly transcendent deity through contrast with a mythical world which was in fact only a deification of existing mundane reality.

Another relevant point might be the unitary and cumulative character of the biblical story, to which we referred earlier. I have the impression that myths do not form a sequence with unity: there are more and more myths, and when we come to the end of one we find another, but they do not form a sequence, except perhaps when mythographers have drawn them together, for example in Philo of Byblos.[9] This might indeed mean that the story character of the Bible does after all differentiate it from myth, and perhaps this is what scholars have been groping after when they have said that the Bible is history and not myth. This of course is not to say that all non-sequential narratives should count as myth. The parables of Jesus, for instance, are non-sequential, and it makes no sense to discuss whether the Prodigal Son comes 'before' or 'after' the Good Samaritan; but these parables are second-order material, in that they are embedded within the larger framework of the Gospel story as a whole. It is interesting, incidentally, to reflect, in view of the long insistence we have had that *historical* narrative is the typical and central biblical form, that this form was not characteristic of Jesus's own teaching.

We may ask therefore whether the question about the referential nature of myth is not the central one. Is it not the case that the Christian faith asserts that the story of the Bible is referentially meaningful, that is, that there are really existing entities to which it refers; and, similarly, events which have really happened to which it refers, and that this reference, though not exact, is essential? The descriptions are not perfect but the things referred to are really there, and the religion depends on this. But how really are the things all really there? Few believers now believe that (say) hell is really there, in the sense of reality in which God is really there. When people object to the word *myth*, they are stressing the need for the real existence of entities and events referred to in the Bible; when others return to the word *myth*, they are perhaps reminding us that the existence of some such realities does not in itself prove or entail that there is a reality of the same degree of realness corresponding to *every* biblical term. And this is probably granted even by those who most strongly object to the use of the term *myth*.

In conclusion, if we look not just at the Bible as a whole, but at incarnation in particular, there are some small but special points to be made. The discussion of incarnation has been rather heated, it seems, exactly because it has arisen on a mainly Anglican soil where there is a very strong tradition of insistence that incarnation is the central and absolutely essential core of Christian doctrine. An outside observer, say a continental Protestant, might find something paradoxical in the way this works out. He might feel that those who express the greatest abhorrence of the word *myth*, when applied to incarnation, themselves heartily express opinions which, to him, seem to imply that incarnation is – a myth. He might wonder whether the love of the incarnation concept might be not something based uniquely on the doctrine of the Person of Jesus Christ but might be also the symbol of wider and more general convictions about the relation of the divine to the human, in Church and in world; and if the incarnation of Jesus Christ was thus the supreme particular case of a general incarnationalism, he would wonder if that too did not make it a myth. And he would wonder about the acute sensitivity to the historical 'authenticity' of the Gospels in particular, when accompanied with a much lower concern about other portions of Holy Scripture.

Where incarnation is uniquely emphasized, it can lead, though it does not necessarily lead, to a situation where the Church is thought of as beginning with the incarnation, while the Old Testament and its people are relegated to a purely preparatory function. Now this is important because it is to be suspected that, within the Gospels themselves, incarnation is a secondary concept rather than a first-line one. The first-line question about Jesus is whether he is the Messiah expected in Israel. This seems to be the question of the earlier strata. Incarnation, by contrast, may be an interpretation of Messiahship, in the light of the passion and resurrection. In other words, it is not the case that the basic insight of the Gospels is incarnation, which insight is, however, cloaked in time-bound Jewish terminology about the Messiah. I think it is the other way round: the priority lies with the question of the Messiahship. This, if right, could lead to a recognition that incarnation is not absolutely central to the basic strata of the New Testament, and that must imply that Christianity is thinkable without the centrality of incarnation. Whether or not we find it useful to talk about a *myth*, there is here some point of contact or parallelism with those who have thought that incarnation is a myth. For me, however, this would only lead on to the other question: what sort of value do we give to the assertion that Jesus is the Christ, the Messiah of Israel's expectation, and thereby to the traditions of the Old Testament and of Judaism out of which the ideas of that Messiahship arose?

Some Thoughts on Narrative, Myth and Incarnation

NOTES

1. One can also use Hans Frei's terminology and say that the biblical story is 'history-like'; see his *The Eclipse of Biblical Narrative* (1974). His words on the wrong turning taken when this history-like material came to be evaluated for its quality as history are worth quoting: 'The realistic or history-like quality of biblical narratives, acknowledged by all, instead of being examined for the bearing it had in its own right on meaning and interpretation was immediately transposed into the quite different issue of whether or not the realistic narrative was historical' (ibid., p. 16.)

2. Some of the wording of this sentence is indebted to an as yet unpublished paper by my colleague Dr John Barton.

3. Cf. Rachel Trickett, below, p. 38.

4. A. E. Harvey, *Companion to the New Testament (New English Bible)* (1970), p. 312.

5. It should hardly be necessary to point out that this argument has nothing to do with the question of credibility of miraculous acts and the like. That is irrelevant here. The question is not one of the historical actuality of the expulsion of the money-changers, but of at what stage of the story it took place. The apologetic argument that it took place twice is, of course, an explanation that merely makes the incident ludicrous, literarily as well as historically.

6. Geza Vermes's approach to the Gospels as intending to recount history (cf. below, pp. 55–8) is not irreconcilable with my position here, though the terms and emphasis are different. *If* we consider that their purpose was to recount history, and one certainly can speak in that way, then the evidence of their own product shows that they did not do so very exactly, and a critical process is necessary to separate out the elements that are historically probable from those that are less so. Moreover, the meaning of statements in the Gospels about eye-witness testimony and the like have to be understood in the light of the way in which the Gospel writers have actually operated in the whole of their work.

7. It was only after this paragraph was written that I came across the interesting comparison between novels and Barth's mode of biblical interpretation as treated by D. F. Ford, 'Barth's Interpretation of the Bible', in S. W. Sykes, ed., *Karl Barth: Studies of his Theological Method* (1979), especially pp. 71ff, 76–82.

8. G. S. Kirk, *Myth: Its Meaning and Functions in Ancient and Other Cultures* (1970), pp. 187ff.

9. A Greek writer of the first century A.D., cited extensively by Eusebius, who wrote an account of Phoenician myths and legends; see J. Barr, 'Philo of Byblos and his "Phoenician History" ', *Bulletin of the John Rylands University Library*, vol. lvii (1974–5), pp. 17–68.

3

Truth in Christology

JOHN MACQUARRIE

IN philosophy, in the natural and human sciences, in our common sense utterances, we claim that what we are saying is true, and we think we know what we mean by this claim. But when we attempt to say what truth is, we find that this is very difficult and that the topic has been the subject of much controversy. Aquinas, Kierkegaard, and Ayer, to mention only three philosophers, have given vastly different accounts of what is meant by 'true'. I think that at the present time many philosophers have given up, as mistaken, the attempt to find a single concept of truth, the essence of truth, so to speak. They would agree with John Lucas when he declares: 'There is no single criterion of truth. Different disciplines have different criteria, often unspecified, sometimes, where specified, liable to conflict.'[1] Mathematicians, chemists, historians and even, we may hope, theologians, are all in quest of truth, but only confusion results if we seek to impose a uniform concept of truth upon them or uniform criteria for the testing of truth. This diversity at the level of the sciences and intellectual disciplines is reflected in some measure on the level of common sense.

Still, I do not think it is satisfactory just to say that truth is multiform, and leave it at that. There must be at least some 'family resemblance' that makes us speak of truth, and even more importantly, leads us to claim to have arrived at truth in all these diverse inquiries. Let me suggest what this is. We think we have attained to truth when we know things as they really are, or when they are disclosed to us as they are, without concealment or distortion. I must at once add, however, that I am not sure that what I have said would apply in the case of logic and mathematics, where one is dealing with formal truths. But we can leave aside these rather special cases, and say that when one is considering the question of material truths, then, however different the methods and criteria that are appropriate to different subject matters, the goal is in each case to know that subject matter as it really is. This is what the Greeks called *aletheia*, the state of unhiddenness or discoveredness.

When the problem of truth is approached in this way, then I think one has got to make the further assertion that truth has always a

24

personal dimension, that is to say, truth is truth for someone who is capable of receiving truth. Truth implies an intelligence that appropriates the truth. Thus we find Heidegger making the rather startling assertion that 'before Newton's laws were discovered, they were not "true" '.[2] He immediately goes on to say that this does not mean they were false, or that the phenomena uncovered by these laws behaved any differently. But 'through Newton the laws became true; and with them, entities became accessible in themselves to human intelligence'.[3]

It was, of course, this personal dimension of truth that was stressed by Kierkegaard. He did not deny that there are 'objective' truths of fact. These can be written down in books or stored in retrieval systems, and are instantly available to anyone caring to look them up. But there are also truths which can be learned only through 'an appropriation process of the most passionate inwardness'.[4] Kierkegaard has in mind here quite explicitly the truth of Jesus Christ, and the Johannine assertion that he *is* the way, the truth, and the life. The truth here is inseparable from the way. It cannot be read off and instantly appropriated, but can be appropriated only through what Kierkegaard calls 'subjectivity' or 'inwardness'. Admittedly, the use of the word 'truth' here in relation to a person – 'Christ is the truth' – is unusual. But there is something like a parallel in the Reformation teaching that the truth of Scripture is not to be read off from the words and sentences alone, but can be appropriated only through the 'inward testimony of the Holy Spirit'.

It is worth pointing out further that this kind of inward appropriation is not peculiar to the truths of faith but occurs also in scientific discovery. The most famous case is surely that of Archimedes, running out of the baths with his triumphant cry, 'Eureka!' For him, the dis-covering or un-veiling of truth had the force of a revelation. Bernard Lonergan has analysed Archimedes' experience in some detail as a typical case of what he calls 'insight'. I shall mention only the last point in his analysis, his claim that the insight 'passes into the habitual texture of one's mind'.[5] It is here that the parallel with Kierkegaard's talk of 'appropriation' emerges. In both cases, a truth is not simply to be noted in passing; it is to be taken into the mind of the person to whom it is dis-covered, and there it both forms his mentality and becomes the ground of fresh discovery.

When one pays attention to the discovering and appropriation of truth, then truth appears more as an event than a property. We commonly tend to think of truth as if it were a property of propositions, but the primordial truth is the event of discovering things as they really are, even if that discovery is forthwith embodied (and perhaps obscured) in a proposition. Especially in the case of religious faith, it may be virtually impossible to find a form of words that will do

25

anything like justice to the original insight.

But does not this stress on a personal dimension to truth, and, even more, Kierkegaard's use of such terms as 'subjectivity' and 'inwardness', undermine the whole notion of truth as making a claim which, at least implicitly, is a universal claim? Can something be true for me, but not for you? If so, are there as many truths as there are individuals, and have we slipped into a complete relativism or scepticism, in which 'truth' has ceased to be a meaningful expression?

I do not think so. It means only that the question of truth and falsity is a much more complex one than is often supposed. To acknowledge that there is a personal dimension in truth is not to make it an arbitrary matter, or to suggest that a proposition or theory is made true simply because it is believed. Even Kierkegaard, though his emphasis on subjectivity may have been unfortunate, was quite clear that no one can believe nonsense if he understands it to be nonsense. We cannot force ourselves to believe what does not claim us as truth. No doubt it is sometimes the case that we do not want to know the truth. Yet if we are exposed to truth, that is to say, if we know something as it really is, there is a compulsion in that situation. The truth claims us irresistibly, and we can only be docile before it. It is not our believing, or our wanting to believe, that makes something true. Rather, the truth exacts our belief. This is possible because of our nature as cognitive beings, endowed with the capacities for perception, understanding, and judgement. Admittedly, we can also fall into error, for neither our perceptions nor our intellectual operations are infallible. We may accept as true something that eventually turns out to be false. But we do not believe what we know to be false – that very form of words involves a contradiction. We believe that which our minds judge to have a claim to truth. To quote a recurring phrase in the Pastoral Epistles, 'This is a true (*pistos*) saying, and worthy (*axios*) of all men to be received, that Christ Jesus came into the world to save sinners.'

That last clause, 'Christ Jesus came into the world to save sinners', is a christological affirmation, and may serve to remind us that as our theme is truth in Christology, it is time that we turned away from more general considerations to this specific topic. Yet the general discussion should have put us on our guard against looking for any simple answer to the question about truth in Christology. The language of Christology is itself a composite language, in which there are interwoven assertions of different kinds, so that even in this fairly limited area, one has to distinguish different kinds of truths and to employ different criteria for their evaluation.

I think we can distinguish at least three different kinds of affirmation in Christology, and the truth of each of the three kinds needs to be approached in the specific way appropriate to it. First, either explicitly or implicitly, Christology seems to commit us to some straight historical affirmations, as that Jesus Christ lived and died in Palestine at a particular time in history. Second, and more important, there are distinctively theological assertions, like the one already quoted, that Jesus Christ came into the world to save sinners. Third, there seems to be still another type of assertion that is more speculative or even metaphysical, as that Jesus Christ is one in being (*homoousios*) with the Father.

This composite language, it seems to me, reflects the language of gospel itself. I should say that I am using the word 'gospel' here in a broad way, to include not only the four books of the New Testament actually called 'Gospels', but also the 'gospel' as understood by Paul and other New Testament writers as the substance of Christian preaching. We might say that Christology is *gospel that has been reflected upon and criticized*. It is a second-order language which nevertheless reflects the characteristics of the first-order language on which it is directed.

What then is gospel? It has often been claimed that the four books called Gospels constitute a unique literary *genre*, but perhaps it is easier to say what they (and the gospel preached by Paul) are not, rather than what they are. Gospel is not straight history, though it contains or assumes some historical affirmations. Gospel is not straight legend, though it may contain legendary elements. Gospel is not straight theology, though it contains theology and is theologically motivated in a very high degree. Gospel is not straight mythology, but it contains and implies mythology, and the mythology may in turn imply some kind of metaphysic.

The task of Christology is to reflect on, clarify, criticize, and generally try to make sense of this mass of diverse material. I have said that at least three kinds of truth seem to be involved in this, and we shall now examine each in turn.

First of all, there is historical truth, and I think we need not linger over this too long. I do not mean that the question of historical truth in relation to Christology is unimportant, and I would not agree with Kierkegaard's almost contemptuous dismissal of the merely historical as irrelevant. It does seem to me that something vital to both gospel and Christology lies in the assertion of the historical actuality of Jesus and of some basic facts about him. I say 'something vital', for if this is a gospel addressed to men and women living 'in the flesh' and struggling amid the concrete actualities of history, then I think that gospel must itself participate in history.

But I think we can be brief in dealing with the question because the methods of historical investigation are already largely agreed, and are the same whether one is inquiring about Jesus of Nazareth or, let us say, Julius Caesar. So, whatever may be the difficulties on particular issues, historical questions arising out of Christology do fall within an area where, in principle, there are agreed ways of establishing what is true.

From Reimarus and Strauss down to Bultmann in our own time, the historical basis of the Gospels has been subjected to critical and often sceptical examination. Much that was for long supposed to be a record of historical events would have to be categorized as myth or legend by thinking people today. Yet there is a core that is resistant to dissolution – the 'Christ-event', as it is often called nowadays. Like all historical events, it is constituted not just by an individual (in this case, Jesus of Nazareth), but by the whole nexus of human relationships in which he stood and which are a part of him. The modern historian can still discern the main outlines of this event, though he strips from it the supernatural trappings of the traditional accounts. What is revealed is the birth of a new type of society and a new concept of humanity, claiming Jesus as its inspirer. The question is whether this core of historical truth is adequate for the christological superstructure which Christians have built upon it. And here we strike on a curious paradox. It is often supposed that biblical criticism has undermined faith in Jesus Christ. It could be argued, on the contrary, that by slimming him down, so to speak, to the human reality, without supernatural knowledge or supernatural powers, it has made him all the more impressive, at any rate to people in a post-mythical age. History reveals him as a fully human being fully participating in human history and inaugurating a new understanding of humanity. This is more impressive than any miracles or supernatural powers. But is it adequate for all that Christology has wanted to assert about him?

That question brings us to our second type of truth, theological truth. Clearly, the main assertions both of gospel and Christology are not historical assertions, even if they are bound up with some such assertions. That Jesus came into the world to save sinners, that he is the incarnate Word, that God raised him from the dead, and so on – these are not historical assertions, as history is understood nowadays. They are theological assertions, and the truth of theological assertions cannot be assimilated to the truth of historical assertions. What then would count as truth in a theological assertion?

I think we have to turn away at this point from the concepts and criteria of truth that hold in the sciences, whether natural sciences or human sciences (including history, so far as it can claim to be scientific). The kind of truth brought to light in a theological, (or, more specifically, a christological) assertion is more like the truth of art than the truth of science. I am not identifying it with the truth of art, for I think art and theology has each its own kind of truth, but I am claiming that a comparison with the truth of art may be more helpful in leading us to an understanding of truth in Christology than a comparison with truth in the sciences.

Do we have to argue that art is as much concerned with truth as are the sciences? I would have thought that this is a point too obvious to need argument, and it is certainly how many great artists have themselves understood their work. Gadamer, on whom I shall be leaning rather heavily in this part of my essay, declares: 'Art is knowledge, and the experience of the work of art is a sharing in this knowledge. . . . Does not the experience of art contain a claim to truth which is certainly different from that of science, but equally certainly is not inferior to it?'[6] Again, he maintains: 'The esthetic experience is not just one kind of experience among others, but represents the essence of experience itself. . . . An esthetic experience always contains the experience of an infinite whole.'[7]

At this point Gadamer has been much influenced by Heidegger's famous essay, 'The Origin of the Work of Art'. In that essay, Heidegger rejects any subjective theory of art, as if it were chiefly concerned with expressing the mind of the artist. The work of art is concerned rather with the truth of things as they are, with uncovering them and bringing them into the light. We recall that for the Greeks truth was *aletheia*, 'unconcealedness'. Heidegger remarks: 'If we conceive of truth as unconcealedness, we are not merely taking refuge in a more literal translation of a Greek word.' Taking as an illustration a Greek temple, he claims that the two essential features in such a work of art are 'the setting up of a world and the setting forth of the earth'. 'Earth' is the raw material from which the marble has been quarried and is now set forth in the light of day; 'world' is the structure of meaning into which the marble has been brought through its incorporation into the temple, so that now we become aware of its potentialities. In and through the art-work the event of truth happens, like a revelation. The work of art has exposed and brought to light world and earth.[8]

In line with this, we find Gadamer claiming that the artistic representation reveals the truth more than the original which it represents, the work of art more than the material out of which it has been constructed. 'With regard to the recognition of the true,' he writes, 'the being of representation is superior to the being of the material represented, the Achilles of Homer more than the original Achilles.'[9] Such representation is not, of course, a mere copying of the original. It is 'not merely a second version, a copy, but a recognition of the essence'.[10]

It should be added that the truth of art, although it is indeed an event with a personal dimension, is not just subjective or arbitrary. There are canons of taste, and Gadamer claims that 'taste undoubtedly includes a mode of knowing' and that 'taste in its essential nature is not a private but a social phenomenon'.[11]

Let us now ask whether and to what extent this conception of the truth of art can be helpful in clarifying what we might mean by truth in Christology.

We remind ourselves of my provisional definition of Christology as 'gospel that has been subjected to reflection and criticism'. We come back then to the question about the nature of gospel. Can we say that gospel is analogous to an art-work? A gospel does resemble a work of art in the sense that it does not merely copy an original or offer a second version of it, but, dare we venture to say, exposes the essence of the original, so that there takes place the event of truth, the setting forth in unconcealedness of the fundamental meaning and reality of the original? A history of Jesus, if we had been left one, would be a copy or second version of the original – though it would necessarily have been an imperfect copy, since a personal life can never be fully captured in words. But a gospel, one might claim, sets forth what Gadamer calls 'a recognition of the essence'. It does so by weaving together historical incidents, teachings and sayings, mythological ideas, legends, theological reflections, and so on.

The writers of the Gospels may not have been very erudite, but their products are surely analogous to works of art, and in some cases are art-works of genius. The account of the trial of Jesus in John's Gospel is a good example. If there had been a clerk of court who had left us a transcript of the trial, it would probably have read very differently. But John, by what Bultmann calls 'a remarkable inter-weaving of tradition and specifically Johannine narration',[12] has dramatically presented the essential meaning, which is a reversal of the roles of Jesus and his judges, so that it is the political and ecclesiastical establishments that are shown to be on trial.

All works of art are executed in a style that belongs to a particular time and culture. This is true also of the New Testament writings. The ideas and devices used to set forth the significance of Jesus come out of a first-century Near Eastern background, and many of them do not readily communicate with us today. It is remarkable, however, that so much in the New Testament still communicates with us directly, and it is the mark of a great work of art that it can communicate across cultural boundaries. But gospel must pass into Christology, in which, through reflection and criticism, the original insights are being continually renewed and reinterpreted.

It will be remembered that Gadamer claimed that the representation in the work of art is not less but more than the original – the Achilles of Homer is more than the original Achilles, to quote his own example. Are we then committed to saying something similar about Jesus Christ, if we apply the analogy of the art-work to gospel and Christology? Perhaps we are, and this would not be a new departure in theology. It would be something like Kähler's teaching that 'the real Christ is the preached Christ',[13] the Christ presented in the gospel or *kerygma*, not the figure revealed by historical research; or like Kierkegaard's claim that to his contemporaries Jesus was incognito and unrecognizable;[14] or like Barth's startling remark that 'Jesus Christ is also the rabbi of Nazareth, one whose activity is so easily a little commonplace alongside more than one founder of a religion'.[15] After all, there were thousands of people who saw and heard the original Jesus, and who either made no response or responded with hostility. To those who did recognize him as the Christ, he is represented by Matthew's Gospel as saying, 'Flesh and blood has not revealed this to you', or, as we might express it nowadays, 'You have not learned this from empirical observation.'

We could say that the truth of Jesus Christ, like the truth of Newton's laws, only happened with its dis-covery, that is to say, when that truth had been received and appropriated. The Jesus presented in the gospel and in Christology is one who has already been dis-covered. The evangelists have already seen in him a 'glory', to use one of their words. Perhaps now we would say an 'ultimacy'. In Gadamer's language, there has taken place a 'recognition of the essence'.

Let us remind ourselves too that such a recognition is not an arbitrary matter. The New Testament witnesses, like all human beings, had powers of perception, understanding, and judgement. They had in addition the spiritual sensitivity that came from their nurture in the Jewish faith. They believed that a new reality had come to expression in Jesus Christ, and to this they testify in their Gospels.

Can we share their assessment of Jesus, even if we would need to express it differently? Obviously, we are to a large extent dependent on their testimony. Does the proclaimed Christ impinge upon us with the force of a revelation – the revelation of an unconcealed ultimacy? At this point, the other kind of truth, the truth to be reached by historical research, again becomes relevant. Christology is not simply gospel, but gospel subjected to reflection and criticism. We have to ask ourselves whether the Jesus reached by historical research as the human centre and inaugurator of the Christ-event does indeed provide the material for the representation in the gospel, the marble for the temple, to revert to our analogy. Obviously, no amount of historical information could *prove* the point, and to this extent Kierkegaard is correct. But some information might cast serious doubt. It would have to be shown that there is a reasonable degree of continuity. This stipulation is made, of course, on the assumption stated earlier in my essay, that the historical actuality of Jesus is of theological importance, and that even if the gospel can be considered analogous to a work of art, it cannot be regarded as pure fiction or pure mythology.

I pass now to a third type of truth. The processes of reflection and criticism by which the first confessions of faith in Christ were transformed into the relatively sophisticated and systematic statements of

Christology raise new questions about truth. I have in mind especially the more speculative or metaphysical forms which Christology came to assume. Let me say that I think these developments were legitimate, even if they came to have an exaggerated importance in the Church. I agree with Tillich that the honest theologian cannot avoid facing and exploring the metaphysical or ontological implications of his utterances about God, Christ, man, and the world;[16] and though I would not go quite as far as Lonergan, I acknowledge some force in his contention that the images applied to Jesus within a Jewish context needed to be re-expressed in universal concepts derived from philosophy.[17]

The Gospels and other New Testament writings already, by implication, make large claims for Christ, but it is only later that these implications are explored. The New Testament writers testify concretely to the ultimacy that they have known in Christ, but sooner or later someone has got to raise the question about the very *possibility* of God's revealing himself in a hum ᴀ life. Is it possible to conceive that the 'ultimate' can be manifeṣd in finite human form?

This inaugurates a new kind of discussion. To a large extent, it can be carried on *Christo remoto*, to use Anselm's phrase, that is to say, without reference to the concrete case of Jesus Christ. One has got to raise questions of a much more general kind, for instance, about the nature of man and his capacity for the divine, and about the problem of God and his relation to the world. A new vocabulary begins to appear; notice that in the last sentence I have introduced the word 'nature', which with 'substance' and a few other philosophical terms supplied the early Church with a vocabulary for such christological pronouncements as the Chalcedonian definition. We may today want to get away from some of these traditional terms, but the problems themselves do not go away, and as Donald MacKinnon has pointed out, even the simplest affirmation about the relation of Christ to the Father involves us in ontology, and if we find the word 'substance' unacceptable, then we have to find another term that will do the kind of work that the rejected term did.[18]

If it is conceded that Christology does lead us into ontological problems, what kind of truth and what kind of criteria are involved? We seem here to be concerned with a type of truth differing both from historical truth and from the theological truth that we likened to the truth of art. We can call it 'ontological' truth, and perhaps the best way to explain what is meant is to give an example at this point. I have said that Christology raises the question about human nature generally, and, in particular, the capacity of the human for the divine. A phenomenology of man is true to the extent that people can recognize themselves and their possibilities in the theory. It is of obvious interest from a christological point of view that almost all contempor-

ary theories of man, from Marxism at the one end of the spectrum to
Thomism at the other, have been stressing the 'openness' of human
nature and its apparently indefinite possibilities for transcendence.
This is an illustration of a general principle implicit in Christology and
the truth of which can be located and tested with reference to
philosophical theories about the being of man.

Let me briefly summarize. Christology, we have seen, is itself a
composite language, and more than one kind of truth is involved in it.
The central christological assertions, the theological ones, lay claim to
a truth that is comparable to the truth of a work of art. But on the one
side, these central truths need to be related to historical assertions
about Jesus, the truth of which is implicitly assumed in the theology;
and on the other side with ontological claims about God and man, the
truth of which is equally assumed by the theology.

NOTES

1. J. R. Lucas, 'True', *Philosophy*, vol. xliv (1969), p. 184.
2. Martin Heidegger, *Being and Time*, E.T. (1962), p. 269.
3. Heidegger, ibid.
4. Søren Kierkegaard, *Concluding Unscientific Postscript*, E.T. (1941), p. 182.
5. Bernard Lonergan, s.j., *Insight* (1970), p. 4.
6. Hans-Georg Gadamer, *Truth and Method*, E.T. (1975), p. 87.
7. Gadamer, ibid., p. 13.
8. Heidegger, 'The Origin of the Work of Art', *Basic Writings*, E.T. (1978), pp. 170–4.
9. Gadamer, op. cit., p. 103.
10. Gadamer, ibid.
11. Gadamer, ibid., p. 34.
12. Rudolf Bultmann, *The Gospel of John*, E.T. (1971), p. 648.
13. Martin Kähler, *The So-Called Historical Jesus and the Historic Biblical Christ*, E.T. (1964), p. 44.
14. S. Kierkegaard, *Training in Christianity*, E.T. (1941), p. 127.
15. Karl Barth, *Church Dogmatics*, i/1, E.T. (1936), p. 188.
16. Paul Tillich, *Biblical Religion and the Search for Ultimate Reality*, (1955), pp. 7–8.
17. Lonergan, *The Way to Nicea*, (1976), pp. 136–7.
18. D. M. MacKinnon, ' "Substance" in Christology', *Christ, Faith, and History*, ed. S. W. Sykes and J. P. Clayton (1972), p. 288.

4

Imagination and Belief

RACHEL TRICKETT

THE Gospels are narrative that purports to be history. Conscious of
the extraordinary and miraculous nature of the events recorded, the
author of St John's Gospel insists on the authenticity of his account:
'This is the disciple which testifieth of these things, and we know that
his testimony is true.' It is inevitable, then, that they should be read
scrupulously as histories need to be read with all the apparatus of
criticism and scholarship to verify their claims and to try to identify
the actual events and incidents they record. But the Gospels are also
story, and the way in which we read and respond to story is imaginative rather than critical. We believe the story in a different way from
which we believe in the veracity of history: it is the appropriateness of
the narrative to the whole experience which it conveys that lies behind
our sense of its reality. What Coleridge calls the willing suspension of
disbelief is present in the act of reading literature, as it is in the act of
creating it. In what sense can we say that reading the Gospels and
responding to their claims of veracity is an imaginative as much as a
rational activity?

Leaving aside for the moment the claims of the Gospels to record a
unique revelation of the truth which actually occurred in history, their
quality as story is commonly conceded to be extraordinary. The
philosophical cast of John's Gospel impedes his narrative in places,
but high moments like the denial of Peter are as securely placed in this
and in the spare style of Mark as in the highly sophisticated literary
narrative of Luke. If a great writer had wished to invent the career of
an incarnate God, he could hardly have contrived effects of greater
vividness than the story the evangelists claim to be recording as fact.
The penultimate chapter, the journey to Jerusalem, the Last Supper,
the agony in the garden, the trial and crucifixion, has a tragic inevitability, a structure which hardly seems consonant with myth or with a
communally developed series of beliefs and traditions about a historical figure whose real status may be in doubt, but who inspired his
followers to think of him as God. Indeed to anyone concerned with
writing fiction, the structure of the narrative and the nature of the
episodes, the vivid distinction of characters, and the sense of human
reality in the gospel records is baffling, since we are to conceive of

them as not having been composed by literary masters. It is these qualities, even in Mark, which predispose the mind to concede a kind of truth to them which is *at least* as true as that we find in Shakespeare's plays or Tolstoy's novels. It is this very vividness and 'reality' that makes it so urgent a matter for the agnostic as much as for the believer to try to decide on the gospel claim to be actual historical fact. The magnificent story purports to be what really happened. In its form in the Gospels it bears little relation to the picaresque legends of the Hindu gods, or the mixture of law-giving and episode in the Koran. There are many passages where Jesus is presented as the teacher dispensing rabbinical wisdom; there are the stories within a story of the parables; there are the direct references to and quotations from Scripture which relate the Gospels to Jewish traditions of the time; but the main plot, as it were, is kept before us constantly by each of the evangelists. Thus it would be hard for the most inveterate doubter to dispute that the evangelists (in composing their record so that from among many other episodes, miraculous acts and reputed sayings of Jesus which must by then have accumulated, the strange and tremendous story of his life stands out clear) were not writing under some form of inspiration.[1]

If the story ended with the crucifixion there would be few who would care to doubt its veracity, give or take some details which might look like the accretion of legend. Jesus is now commonly accepted as a historical figure, a wise teacher, a dedicated being with the power to command human devotion. His death by crucifixion, making allowances for the miraculous overtones as the delusions of his proselytizing followers, is even politically convincing. The problem comes in the last chapter, the final episode. It is the resurrection that throws all in question; as it is the resurrection that is the *raison d'être* of the narrative to the narrators. If Christ be not risen our faith is vain. But to believe as actual truth what looks like the most irrational reversal of the laws of nature, one must again exercise the imaginative comprehension which grasps its appropriateness to the kind of reality the whole of Jesus's life and teaching, like some great literary structure, seems intended to convey.

The attempt to deal with the horrifying fact of death, to come to terms with it, to reconcile the knowledge of its universal inevitability with our innate imaginative incapacity to conceive of ourselves ending, has been a concern of myth and poetry from earliest times. The ancients with their ghost world, their myths like that of Alcestis restored from death by the power of Hercules, in poetic elegy devised a more subtle pattern to typify human horror at loss and the need for some final reconciliation of death with life. The mourning, the calling upon the gods and the powers of nature for consolation, culminates in pastoral elegy in the device of the apotheosis – the dead man himself transformed into a god or a power of nature. And it might look as though Jesus's early followers had used this pattern in their narrative, changing the man Jesus into the god Christ. But the whole point of their message, their contention, is precisely the opposite: that it was only *because* Jesus was god incarnate[2] that the physical resurrection could take place, resurrection being the ultimate manifestation of his divinity and of the relationship of that divinity to humanity. The resurrection is the only major episode in the gospel story (apart from St Luke's account of the nativity) which has any of the quality of myth about it. The authors of *The Myth of God Incarnate* are, it seems to me, really writing about the myth of the resurrection – the incarnation being the prerequisite of that event.

The resurrection is the last event in a chain of circumstances that purport to follow the ordinary course of cause and effect except for those miraculous acts which stand in deliberate contrast to the rational and plausible narrative of Jesus's life history. But we are required by the evangelists to accept this last episode, the ultimate miracle, as a rational conclusion to the story. It seems, indeed, against reason to do so.

One way, at least, of approaching this problem, is to try to think of how we react to episodes and events of an extraordinary or significant kind in any *fictional* narrative as at least some sort of analogy. We commonly and too loosely use the word 'symbolic' of any circumstance in a narrative that seems to us especially significant. This is often as imprecise as the frequent use of the word 'myth' for a significant story. If the word symbol means a dissociated circumstance or sign standing for something else, then it is a figure singularly inappropriate for a prose narrative which purports to be a rational account of quotidian experience; and this, traditionally, is what fiction or narrative as a literary form sets out to do. Poetry and drama concentrate the time element, to some extent distort it for the purposes of emphasis; even the poetic epic tends to juggle with time-scheme in order to underline its themes. But the rhythm of the novel imitates that of our own day-to-day experience; and in such a form of narrative, as in history itself, normal sequence with its concomitant implications of cause and effect is the predominant treatment of time. In Tolstoy's *Anna Karenina*, when Vronsky's horse stumbles in the race and is killed Anna drops her opera-glasses and for the first time Karenin understands the situation, and many critics have declared the moment to be symbolic. A better term would be *omen*: it is an ominous moment. The circumstance points forward to the inevitable outcome of Anna's love for Vronsky, and in doing so it adumbrates what was basically at fault in the relationship. Thus it is especially appropriate to the texture of narrative for it looks back as well as forward, it recalls origins and predicts consequences.

Many of the events in the Gospels seem to me to be of this nature. Their plausibility in the context of story is inevitably connected with their position in a causal chain. The occasions when Jesus pronounces himself to be more than purely human, or when others so pronounce him, are moments of enlightenment or revelation which are not symbolic or mythic so much as realizations of what certain events, recorded as fact – the obscure birth, the meeting with John the Baptist, the miracles – adumbrate.[3] At the same time they contain within themselves the prediction of the outcome of such realizations – the passion and the resurrection.

The Gospels openly make use of this narrative resource. Jesus is seen as fulfilling the prophecies; the Old Testament stories are realized and comprehended in his life and actions. In the Old Testament itself, lives and actions are continually seen as representing certain great truths about the relationship of man and God; to take a few at random, the sacrifice of Isaac, the wanderings of Israel, the dedication of the priestly child Samuel, whose mother's hymn of thanksgiving anticipates the Magnificat. When I put it in that way I am open to the criticism that the author of Luke's Gospel was deliberately recalling Hannah's hymn of thanksgiving (as of course he was) in writing the Magnificat. But in a narrative or story sense, this anticipation in one story and recapitulation or fulfilment in another, is not a mythological or symbolic process so much as a sequential narrative device, a matter of origins and outcomes, a weaving of the story of continuous human experience in relation to God bearing a direct relation to mundane reality.

But for this to be 'significant' it must possess historical and actual plausibility. The stories of the Old Testament, with the exception of the story of the Fall and perhaps that of the Flood, have precisely this plausibility. It is what distinguishes them from a great allegory like *Pilgrim's Progress*. They purport to be history; the history of God's dealings with his chosen people the Jews, and in the same way the gospel narratives (especially the Synoptics) purport to be historical and actual. It is clear even from their supernatural elements that their claim is to be taken as historical. The supernatural quality of miracles, for instance, can only be of extraordinary significance in a normal historical context. The magical happenings of a romance or allegory are part of a symbolic structure and cannot be, in the same way, signs or miracles. The significance of the miraculous depends not on an acceptance of the magical, but on a basic acquiescence in the normal and rational.

We can, therefore, see that the authors of the Gospels wrote their narratives in the form of chronicles – recognizable as like the Old Testament records, part of the continuing story of God's dealings with his people. This is so, as it is true that if they wished to accept or further Jesus's claim to be the Son of God they must necessarily present him as the last in the line of the chosen, the prophets: He that is to come. Such claims are not made for the characters in Old Testament narratives, but those figures look forward, as the whole Jewish people did, to the fulfilment of the prophecies, to the advent of the Messiah. There are, of course, types in the Old Testament, imaginative, symbolic creations like the figure of the Suffering Servant in Isaiah who are not treated historically, but were clearly devised to demonstrate the nature of divine mercy and humility. Jesus in the Gospels is treated as historically as any of his Old Testament predecessors, and he is seen as their culmination, but claims are also made for him which relate him to the mythical figure of the Suffering Servant, and the final episode of his life, the resurrection, though recorded as history, shares something of that quality of myth which we find in the story of the Fall. Yet in the Acts and the Epistles this same event is presented to us as historically and actually true, and one upon which the whole of the Church's faith depends.

Two kinds of truth are interwoven in the gospel narratives – the historical and the imaginative, and we are required to respond to each and to both together. The evangelists are concerned to verify the story of the empty tomb, countering the anxious arguments of the high priests and of subsequent doubters. The resurrection appearances[4] in Luke and John are emphatic in their underlining of the physical fact of it: Thomas's declaration of his doubt and its resolution; the disciples on the Emmaus road seeing Jesus break the bread and knowing him in that action. Only John's account of the appearance of Jesus by the lake of Galilee has about it a sort of eeriness which seems to exist in the no-man's land between actuality and dream. Yet in all these accounts the sense of mystery and the sense of reality are both strongly and simultaneously present. Jesus's injunction to Mary Magdalene not to touch him seems as natural as his sudden appearance in the upper room to answer Thomas's demand seems mysterious. In all these episodes the two kinds of truth are inextricably interwoven, and we are required to accept both.

The way in which we assent to all this, the way we entertain it in our minds imaginatively and rationally has not been often enough considered in my view. Scholars, and often the clergy in relation to the laity, are peculiarly reluctant to concede the innate human capacity to accept the marvellous, to delight in wonder and respond to the strongest claims made on the imagination. Artists, by contrast, must always assume it; the justification of their work depends upon it. It is curious to notice this reluctance today, and how it extends to a profound distrust of the beauty and power of language as if it were inevitably an enemy of the truth, one of the more dangerous causes of the present enthusiasm for retranslating Scripture and revising liturgies. It is dangerous because the act of consenting or believing, like any act of the will, involves that quality of imagination which can entertain and hold in the mind the completeness of a complex truth with all its many facets. It is this quality that is delighted by good literature, responding to the extraordinary capacity of the writer to complete and make a whole pattern out of fragmented human experience. To see truth as a process of stripping bare, paring away, is a common rational perception; to see truth as a gathering together, a process of accretion which may appear to lead to paradox and contradiction, but which, in the end, resolves them by asserting completeness, is a function of the imagination.

To the modern mind the truth of narrative is easier to entertain than the truth of poetry. The novel is the one 'modern' form of literature, and its appearance in the eighteenth century as a form which purports to be authentic, a kind of history (the titles of the earliest novels often run thus – *The History of Tom Jones; a Foundling*), seems to reflect the post-Cartesian spirit of the times, the need to verify by the *thinking* self everything we *experience*. We respond at once to this kind of story; a story of everyday not of the marvellous, a story which sustains the illusion of historical reality, and one which follows the rhythm of our day-to-day consciousness. We are often not aware of the implausibility of details if the power of the narrative and the genius of the author are strong enough. This, I think, is part of our difficulty in apprehending the Gospels. As story they are so compelling that we are easily convinced by them and there is little the imagination finds disturbing until the conclusion when we are presented with a miraculous circumstance of a quite different order from the miracles of healing, and asked to accept it in the same way in which we have accepted the rest: that is, as part of a factual narrative, not as a sudden excursus into myth or poetry.

The authors themselves understood the difficulty. How Mark's unfinished Gospel would have ended is still open to speculation, but the empty tomb, at which it breaks off, carries with it, as in the other three Gospels, the sense of shock that is one of the most powerful effects of all in carrying conviction. Some have believed in the authenticity of the resurrection because of the realism of a detail – John's outrunning Peter to get to the tomb first in the Fourth Gospel, for instance – but the question of what and why we believe when we come to the end of this record, is very much involved with the way *in which* we believe. The narrative structure of the Gospels (as well as the conviction of their authors) *requires* us to accept the final episode as fact. This is the last chapter of the novel, the dénouement, the resolution; if it doesn't work, the whole book is flawed. Everything, the imagination insists, must hang together, must demonstrate a peculiar kind of appropriateness, the sense of which is one of the true marks of genius in a writer.

It might help to clarify the nature of the conviction the Gospels expect from us if we turn to Coleridge, whose subtle and powerful mind often pondered the problem of belief. In his annotations to the *English Divines* he inevitably touches frequently on the nature of belief. He was obsessed by the notion that the great seventeenth-century Anglican divines whom he loved, on the one hand had unduly minimized the importance of the critical approach to the Gospels in favour of an appeal to patristic tradition (and Coleridge was no fundamentalist in his approach to Scripture); on the other hand, and paradoxically, in doing so, they had failed to grasp the role of imagination and the intuitive faculty in understanding the great religious concepts of original sin and the need for salvation. It is interesting to discover that here Coleridge finds Calvin and especially Luther more imaginatively compelling, more aware of men's profounder feelings. 'This (I should say of Original Sin) is mystery. We do not so properly *believe* it as *know* it.' What Coleridge means here, I think, is that we have experienced it in the way an artist experiences his material before he begins to express it. The very deep sense of imperfection which is rooted in human beings is left unsatisfied and unresolved by a religion which cannot account for it, or solace it, or which tries to ignore it. To Coleridge it would have seemed a mark of the superficiality of our age that the Church has turned its back on the notion of original sin and tried as much as possible to eliminate from the liturgy any references to it. For man's sense of sin is inextricably associated with his sense of righteousness, and to Coleridge each was something that human beings *know*, *experience*, are profoundly *aware* of. He was loath to give up a rational acceptance of the story of the Fall because of St Paul's use of it; nevertheless, his instinct was to see it as a 'mythos' which he proceeds to define thus: 'The literal fact you could not comprehend if it were related to you; but you may conceive of it as if it had taken place thus and thus.'

But the 'mythos' of the resurrection in the Gospels is presented to us as literal fact, and thus to believe it requires something more even than imagination. It requires faith. 'Faith', Coleridge writes, 'is not an accuracy of logic, but a rectitude of heart.' Those who write about the myth of God incarnate are not occupying themselves with the central problem of the nature of faith, the kind of act belief involves. They rely on 'accuracy of logic' to discover what is possible in historical and rational terms, or what can be translated into twentieth-century language, about a revelation to understand which we might say in the words of Paulina from the end of *The Winter's Tale*: 'It is required you do awake your faith.' The gospel narratives demand that we must believe that an action occurred within time and history that cannot be grasped by purely temporal and historical judgement.

Coleridge was deeply aware of the reality of the Christian doctrine, its closeness to human experience. 'The man who cannot see the redemptive agency in creation', he writes, 'has but a dim apprehension of the creative forces.' And again, relying more on St Paul than on the formulation of the creeds, he writes: 'Can words in the Creed be more express than those of St Paul to the Colossians, speaking of Christ as *the creative mind of his Father*, before all worlds, begotten before all things created?' It was perhaps natural that Coleridge, as a poet, should be so strongly aware of the creative power in the redeeming role Jesus claims for himself in the Gospels. To Coleridge, who began as a Unitarian and ended as an orthodox Christian, it seemed increasingly *appropriate* to the nature of reality as he had grasped it, that God's temporal manifestation in history to save his beloved but flawed creature, should at one and the same time occur in a recognizable pattern of historical circumstance, and yet transcend that pattern to reveal a super-temporal truth, still within the limits of actual human experience.

Everyone makes the act of faith – or of denial – in his own way. This essay is merely an attempt to suggest that the stupendous claims of the gospel narratives need to be weighed not only against scholarly and historical analysis, but against the kind of truth which appertains to the imagination and to the creative activity. If we look at them in this way we shall see that the records of the life of Jesus cut across our categorizations and simplifications, and, like our experience of life itself, involve many kinds of rational and imaginative response. To limit the role of imagination simply to art or literature is characteristic of the sort of pedantry which dogs theology or literary criticism as academic disciplines. The human imagination, as much as the human heart or the human mind, has a full part in the whole activity of believing, and it is especially the imagination's sense of appropriateness and of completion that, in my view, allows it to accept the last episode of the Gospels as the story itself requires us to.

NOTES

1. I use the term here in a literary rather than a scriptural sense, in so far as that distinction can be made.
2. I believe this is the implication of the Gospels, but it is not beyond dispute.
3. Biblical scholars today have disputed, it must be said, the historicity of these recorded claims of Jesus.
4. There is, however, considerable dispute about the historicity of the accounts of the resurrection appearances.

41

5

Christology and the Evidence of the New Testament

ANTHONY HARVEY

'IT is essential that the doctrinal theologian recognizes the real position with which he has to deal. He has to recognize that the kind of information about Jesus that theology has so often looked to New Testament scholars to provide is not available.' These words of Maurice Wiles[1] well represent what has come to be regarded almost as an axiom of Christian theology. It is widely assumed today that the result of over a century of critical study of the Gospels has been to call into doubt the very possibility of reliable historical knowledge about Jesus of Nazareth. Form-criticism (it is believed) has demonstrated that both the narratives and the teaching in the Gospels have been so influenced by the needs and concerns of the early Church (which for its own purposes selected, moulded, embellished, and even on occasion supplemented the information it possessed about Jesus) that we can no longer be sure of the reliability of any single report they contain; moreover, so diverse and divergent are the many 'lives' and representations of Jesus which have been composed during the last 150 years, all of which claim to be based on the evidence of the New Testament, that it must be as clear to any dispassionate observer today as it was to Albert Schweitzer more than half a century ago that all these portraits are no more than a reflection of the prejudices and presuppositions of their makers. An objective picture based on the New Testament evidence is clearly unobtainable; the foundations of Christology now have to be laid elsewhere.

This view of the matter is not without justification. It is certainly true that form-criticism has fundamentally affected the methods and the expectations of every student of the New Testament. Once it is granted (and this at least is demonstrable) that relatively short passages in the Gospels once had an independent existence outside their present contexts, and once the assumption is made (which is at least highly probable) that the selection of these passages, their assimilation to certain 'forms', their assignment to a particular moment or context in the ministry of Jesus, and even certain details of their content, may be due to the needs, interests, and purposes of the Church which originally preserved the memory of these things, then the conclusion seems to follow that there is no single verse of the Gospels which is not in principle susceptible of such an analysis. Every report about Jesus becomes suspect as a product, not of authentic reminiscence, but of subsequent reflection. When to this analysis is added the more recent discipline of 'redaction criticism', such that allowance has to be made, not only for the concerns of the Church, but for the theological interests and literary preferences of each individual evangelist, it would seem that the prospects of retrieving any firm historical information from such a complicated process of transmission have receded still further. The theologian can be pardoned for jumping to the conclusion that the results of a century of critical study of the New Testament have been (from the point of view of our knowledge about Jesus) wholly negative.

It is certainly true that for a time New Testament scholars themselves were ready to acknowledge that the consequence of using their new methods might well turn out to be nothing less than a radical scepticism about the possibility of secure historical knowledge of Jesus. The most influential of the form-critics, Rudolf Bultmann, gave vivid expression to this mood (though his own motives were perhaps primarily philosophical) when he devoted only the first thirty pages of his great *New Testament Theology* to the person of the historical Jesus, before proceeding to find a basis for Christian faith in the post-resurrection experience of the apostles. It is not surprising that dogmatic theologians, in their search for a firm starting-point for systematic theology, should have been rapidly forced to the conclusion that New Testament study would henceforth offer them no purchase on the historical facts about Jesus; and the same tone of scepticism has been registered and adopted by an ever widening circle of lay inquirers. It is therefore all the more important to draw attention to the fact that in recent years New Testament scholars (largely unnoticed, it seems, even by other theologians) have been retreating substantially from the extreme of historical scepticism which was reached a generation ago, and that the majority of them today might well not agree that no materials are available in the New Testament for constructing a Christology. Indeed, it seems an urgent matter to offer a more up-to-date and realistic account of the present mood of New Testament scholarship, and to suggest ways in which historical research may still have a part to play in strengthening Christian faith.

For some years now, for example, it has been realized that radical scepticism about the historical value of the information contained in the Gospels rests upon a logical fallacy. It may indeed be true that, in the light of modern critical study, there is virtually no single report of any of the words and deeds of Jesus of which we can be certain, and there is indeed quite a large number of them which are likely to be either fictitious or fashioned by the tradition into something very different from the original. But it does not follow from this that we can know nothing for certain about Jesus. Your estimate of a respected friend or teacher will normally be based on a large number of pieces of information about him, all, or virtually all, of which seem to add up to the kind of personality and achievement which is worthy of respect. Of course it may happen that one of these stories about him turns out to have no basis in fact, and that another has grown considerably in the telling; and you may have to admit that, at least in theory, the same could be true of any of the others. But if so, you will not immediately abandon all possibility of reliable information about this person and transfer your respect elsewhere. What impresses you is the fact that there is so much information which all points in the same direction and allows you to infer a character of consistency and integrity. The mere possibility that any particular source of information may turn out to be unreliable would certainly not lead you to think that you could no longer make any reasonable judgement about him at all. And so it is in modern New Testament study. Attention has moved away from establishing the truth or falsity of any particular report about Jesus, and is now directed more towards the impression made by the narrative as a whole. Writers who string together stories which are devised purely to give credit to the hero will succeed only in presenting a one-sided description of his character, lacking in any real depth or originality; others who are content to collect any anecdotes regardless of historical plausibility will fail to portray a character of any consistency. Neither fault can be laid to the charge of the evangelists. The Jesus who emerges from their accounts has both originality and consistency – the apocryphal gospels, which present by comparison a cardboard figure, offer an instructive contrast. Unless these authors were the most consummate and imaginative artists, able to create a striking and consistent character out of scanty and unreliable sources, we have no alternative but to conclude that the portrait of Jesus which they offer was inspired by, and in broad outlines at least must correspond with, the Jesus who actually existed. It is no accident that in the world of scholarship attention has shifted away from the examination of isolated units of tradition towards the assessment of the cumulative weight of diverse testimonies which all point in the same direction. To this extent at least, few New Testament scholars today would wish to say that we can have no reliable knowledge about Jesus.

Furthermore, it is important to be clear about what we mean by 'certainty' and 'reliability'. It is possible that the whole question of the nature and reliability of our information about Jesus has been subtly distorted by the circumstances in which it was first raised. It is true that for the greater part of the history of Christianity the statements of fact contained in the Bible have seemed to enjoy a quite exceptional degree of certainty: their truth (it was believed) was guaranteed by the divine inspiration of Scripture. Take, for example, the statement in

Mark that Jesus entered the territory of the Gerasenes[2] and there encountered the demoniac called Legion. Until modern times, no one would have doubted the truth of this statement: even the fact that Matthew's Gospel seems to offer a different version of the place-name[3] was one which it was felt must have an easy explanation. But modern topographical study has made it clear that, as it stands, Mark's statement *cannot be correct*. The great Hellenistic city of Gerasa lay far inland from the Sea of Galilee, and possessed no territory on the shore where this incident could have taken place; even Gadara (another city with which it might have been confused) lay some distance away. We can tell from the variations in the manuscript readings[4] that even in antiquity some difficulty was felt about the question, and today most scholars would agree that no certain answer is available. Indeed, the whole inquiry now seems somewhat gratuitous. There is no reason to think that the author of Mark's Gospel was well acquainted with the geography of Galilee and the Decapolis. Gerasa he will have heard of, since it was the largest city immediately to the east of the lake. That its territory did not include the shore was probably not known either to him or to his readers. But nor would it have seemed of great consequence. His purpose was not to achieve geographical precision but to indicate the character and approximate position of the region Jesus had entered. The famous name of Gerasa will have served this purpose well – better, in fact, than an obscure name which might have been more accurate. As we learn to know his methods, we now feel we are getting to know and understand his Gospel better. But if we ask how reliable is the historical information he offers us, we have to confess that it enjoys none of that splendid certainty which it once seemed to derive from the doctrine that the truth of all statements in the Bible is guaranteed by divine inspiration.

But in fact such uncertainty need be a cause for dismay only when it is contrasted with the supernaturally guaranteed certainty which seemed to be offered on the earlier understanding of the authority of Scripture. The appropriate comparison is not with statements which may be believed true on divine authority, but with other historical statements made on the basis of comparable evidence. What we have to ask is not whether a given statement is true with a kind of metaphysical certainty, but whether the fact which it reports may be regarded as at least as well established as other facts which come down to us from antiquity. Some scholars, it is true, are inclined to regard the gospel narratives as inherently 'unhistorical' on the grounds that the facts which they offer us are already so heavily interpreted in the light of Christian experience that we can no longer recover the 'history' which lies behind the interpretation.[5] It is certainly the case that the Gospels tell their story in such a way that it possesses already a profound Christian significance. To this extent they are partial witnesses, and we cannot imagine that the original events always took place just as they record them, still less that they were immediately invested with the significance they took on later. But again it is a mistake to contrast the admittedly heavily interpreted gospel record with an imaginary ideal of objective, completely uninterpreted 'history'. Such history is never in fact written. Bare objective facts exist only, if at all, in archives and account books. History is what makes sense of this raw material by a complex process of selection, arrangement, and interpretation. The Gospels must be compared, not with a hypothetical uncontaminated list of bare events (which would in any case be devoid of significance for religious purposes) but with other historical writings which come down to us from antiquity, and in which too we have to allow for the interpretative bias of their authors. On this test, we shall find that the information about Jesus which we can derive from the Gospels enjoys a high degree of historical reliability. The Gospels can be subjected to investigation with all the tools and methods of modern historical study, and come remarkably well out of the process. So far as their historical reporting is concerned, they bear comparison with the work of any ancient historian, and at many points the information they offer is not merely credible but impressive.

However, it is not merely on general grounds that scholars would now claim to be able to extract from the Gospels reliable information about Jesus. It has become increasingly clear that the methods perfected by form-critics and redaction critics cannot be applied indiscriminately to any passage in the Gospels, and that some parts of the tradition have a much stronger claim to authenticity than others. It has been realized that it is possible to devise criteria for distinguishing between those reports which are more and those which are less likely to go back to Jesus. If, for example, a saying is recorded in a number of different contexts; or if (better still) an item of information is mentioned *en passant* in one context that is also recorded elsewhere; then there is a strong presumption that it is due, not to the creative reflection of the early Church or of the evangelist, but to the strength of a reminiscence going back to the time of Jesus himself. One criterion in particular has proved itself both legitimate and fruitful. This is the principle of 'dissimilarity',[6] which might be crudely described as the axiom that 'odd is true'. If a particular saying or episode is unparalleled in either Jewish or Hellenistic literature, and if there seems to be no possible motive which would have caused the first generation of Christians to attribute such a thing to Jesus, then far the most likely explanation of its presence in the gospel record would seem to be that it was said or done by Jesus himself. By the use of this criterion it has been possible to build up a substantial body of information about Jesus which has a strong claim to authenticity. This information is of course still vulnerable in detail. Our sources of information about the religion and culture of the period are few and patchy (compared, for example, with Rome or Alexandria), and the fact that a saying of Jesus is 'unparalleled' may be due to nothing more than the purely fortuitous absence of any occasion for its mention in the sources we possess; indeed, it has happened more than once that an idiom which was thought to be peculiar to the Gospels has been shown by recent discoveries to have had a wide currency at the time. And not only is this information vulnerable to future research and discovery; it runs the danger of eccentricity. If the object is to build up an authentic portrait of Jesus, this clearly cannot be done by assembling traits which can be identified only by their peculiarity. We need to know not only the respects in which Jesus was totally unlike other people, but also the extent to which he fitted into and was characteristic of his surroundings.

This last point can be developed further. No one who has the task of communicating a message and initiating a movement can afford to speak and act in totally unprecedented ways. In order for his message to be intelligible and his style of leadership to be effective he must work within the conventions and expectations of those to whom he addresses himself: his language and his style of action, however creative and innovatory, must still be intelligible to those who seek to attend to him, and this can be the case only if they can situate him in relation to concepts and categories which are already familiar. To take a simple example: there can be no doubt that Jesus was recognized in his own time as a prophet. Those who encountered him must therefore have discerned in him a number of those qualities and attributes which belonged to the traditional idea of a prophet, to be able to identify him as such. Jesus, in his turn, must have been conditioned and prepared to act within the constraints imposed by this role of prophet, in order that his contemporaries should be able to grasp what kind of person they had to do with, even though he also had the ability to transcend this role and ultimately to impress his followers as 'more than a prophet'. It follows that if our sources allow us to form a clear picture of what the role of prophet amounted to in Jesus's time and culture, we can gain thereby sound information on at least the parameters within which Jesus's work and character were formed, and will then have a framework of normality in which to set those exceptional characteristics which can be at least provisionally established by the use of the criterion that 'odd is true'.

It is from this perspective that it can now be said that recent research has made possible a positive advance in the study of the New Testament. Archaeological discoveries made since the war, and the application of modern critical methods to the study of the large body of post-biblical Jewish literature which exists in Greek and other languages, have made it possible to give new precision to many of the terms and concepts which are found in the Gospels. To give only a few examples: it used to be suspected by sceptical historians that the name Nazareth was an invention by the early Christians in the interests of relating Jesus to such Old Testament concepts as a 'Nazarite' or as the 'branch' (*netser*) which Isaiah had prophesied would stem from Jesse; the name Nazareth occurred nowhere outside Christian literature, and there was no evidence that the modern town of Nazareth existed in the time of Jesus. But in 1955 excavations under the Church of the Annunciation in Nazareth showed that the site was occupied long before the first century A.D., and in 1961 an inscription was found clearly referring to a town of this name. Again, until recently we possessed a large number of literary and more or less rhetorical accounts of crucifixions carried out by the Romans, but the details recorded in the gospel narratives were without any known parallel, and it was open to any critic to argue that these details were due to pious meditation on certain Old Testament texts rather than to any historical reminiscence. But in 1970 a skeleton was found in a Jewish burial ground on the Mount of Olives, belonging to the first century A.D. and showing clear evidence of crucifixion: a nail had been driven through the anklebones to fasten them to a wooden upright, and the legs had been broken by a transverse blow. By this single discovery the gospel accounts of Jesus's crucifixion have been shown to be something other than pious legend: they contain sober reporting of plausible historical fact. The Dead Sea Scrolls, again, have greatly extended our knowledge of the character of a Jewish sect in the time of Jesus, and have given new distinctness to the options which will have been open to anyone who sought to be a teacher and a religious leader – quite apart from having provided striking Jewish parallels to a number of idioms in John's Gospel which had been previously thought to be 'Hellenistic'. As for Jewish literature, though the evidence of important connections with the New Testament has been known for centuries, it is only recently that scientific study of the sources has made it possible to assess the relevance of (for example) the definition of the offence of blasphemy in the Mishnah to the charge allegedly brought against Jesus before the Sanhedrin, or the value of the Jewish 'Testaments' (preserved only in Greek through the work of Christian copyists) as independent evidence for contemporary Jewish beliefs about life after death or the messianic hope.

In these and many other ways our knowledge of the world in which Jesus lived has made and is still making considerable advances, and allows us to give new content and precision to those general statements about Jesus which are known with as much certainty as is the case with any notable figure of the ancient world, but which had previously seemed too vague and colourless to yield significant information. Among examples of such statements we may list the following:[7]

1. Jesus was active mainly in two rather different Jewish environments (Galilee and Judaea) and to a much lesser extent in areas less heavily populated by Jews (the region of Tyre and the Decapolis). There is no record of his having entered any of the pagan towns in Palestine (such as Tiberias) that had been founded in Hellenistic or Roman times. Our knowledge of this limited environment now enables us to form some conception of the style, the conventions, and the language with which he must have worked.

2. There can be no doubt that Jesus was a 'teacher'. But among people whose religion, culture, morality, and civic life – quite apart from their system of criminal justice and civil litigation – were governed by the unquestioned authority of a divinely authorized and immutable code of Law, the sphere of activity and the possibilities for creative innovation open to any teacher were strictly limited. Precisely what stance Jesus adopted towards the Law of Moses, and how he related his own teaching to it, are questions which have long been in dispute among scholars and are by no means settled today. But at least it is now possible to narrow the range of possible answers and define the limits within which Jesus's teaching must have been set if it were to seem intelligible and practicable to his hearers. Our knowledge is now sufficient for the bare statement that Jesus was a teacher to assume both content and significance.

3. It can be said with equal certainty that Jesus was credited with miraculous cures. A large number of testimonies, not all of them Christian, point in this direction. Given the large number of miracle stories which (it was said) were circulating in antiquity, it used to be felt that the exorcisms and cures attributed to Jesus could best be explained as the kind of legendary accretions which inevitably clustered around the story of a notable religious figure. But a closer study of the sources reveals that these 'miracles' were far less common than used to be thought, and that those ascribed to Jesus, far from being the typical feats of a popular charismatic figure, were for the most part without precedent in his own culture, and evince a style of activity that demands serious explanation. Even if (as many would argue) the gospel stories of Jesus's miraculous cures may have grown in the telling, there remains a kernel of irreducible information which must be taken account of in any reconstruction of his work and message.

4. I have already remarked that Jesus was known as a prophet. This is attested not only by numerous instances in the Gospels (which are made the more cogent by the fact that Jesus was never so referred to by Paul or other early Christian writers), but, by implication, by non-Jewish sources as well. The essence of a prophet is that he relates

his message to a specific moment in history, and invests the moment at which he is delivering it with particular significance. There is abundant evidence in the Gospels that this was at least part of the style adopted by Jesus. It has always caused difficulties to those concerned (as the Church has usually been concerned) to draw from the teaching of Jesus timeless truths and precepts valid at any time and place; but recent studies of the nature of prophecy in the culture which Jesus inherited, and of the sociological phenomenon of messianic expectation in general, have helped us to grasp the significance of this prominent feature of Jesus's activity.

5. There can be equally little doubt that Jesus was from first to last a controversial figure. The very large number of stories of his controversies with authorized exponents of the Law cannot be without some historical foundation, and show him to have been expert in matters of detailed interpretation of Scripture. Taken on its own, this is unremarkable. Disagreements on the meaning and application of the Law were the daily occupation of many of Jesus's contemporaries. But it becomes significant when combined with Jesus's other roles. It was no part of the work of a prophet to get involved in legal definitions; it was no part of the work of a legal expert to give warnings of imminent catastrophe. It was precisely Jesus's combination of those roles which was unprecedented, and which offers us highly significant information about him.

6. Jesus's teaching was focused, not upon his own status and function, but upon what he referred to again and again as the reign of God. This concept was known to his contemporaries, but (so far as our sources allow us to judge) was not widely discussed. Jesus's concentration upon it is not only unprecedented; it led him to make use of a large number of idioms in connection with it which he appears to have coined himself. This is admittedly a conclusion which must be advanced with caution. If we had more literature from the period, or if we knew more of the language and idioms in which people actually talked to each other on religious subjects at the time, we might find Jesus's characteristic ways of speaking less remarkable. Nevertheless, his evident concern for the reign of God, almost to the exclusion of discussion of his own status and destiny, remains an important piece of unimpeachable information about him.

7. Finally, it may be said that there are few facts which come to us from the ancient world so well attested as the statement that Jesus was crucified. But this is also a statement which is capable of sustaining an impressive chain of historical inference. It implies that he was executed by the Romans on a charge of sedition, but was 'handed over' to the Roman authority by the Jewish leaders. This was an exceptional step which would have been taken by them only if their own legal procedures and competence were for one reason or another

not adequate to deal with an offender whom they believed it necessary
to have removed from their midst; from which we can infer information about the character of Jesus's activity and teaching – that it was
seriously threatening even if not actually illegal according to Jewish
law – which gives us a criterion for assessing the historicity of many of
the episodes in the Gospels.

This list is by no means exhaustive. One might add, for example,
the well-authenticated reports of the dismay Jesus caused by the
company he kept and by his apparent disregard of the observances
normally expected of a religious teacher; his attitude to children,
unexampled in the ancient world; the importance he evidently attributed to the fellowship of a meal, both for consolidating his own
movement and as a vehicle for religious experience. But enough has
been said to restore to their proper perspective the admitted results of
form- and redaction criticism. It may be granted that a large number
of passages relating to Jesus are now too suspect to be used as evidence
about him. But the quantity of information which is still securely
based – and in some cases more securely than before – is such that we
can justly claim to know as much about Jesus as about almost any
other major personality of the ancient world.

But, it could be argued, nothing that has been said so far is relevant
to Christology. The theologian is not interested in the sheer quantity
of facts which may be known about Jesus. He is interested only in
facts of a particular kind. Professor Wiles's words, with which we
began, are carefully chosen: 'The *kind* of information about Jesus that
theology has so often looked to New Testament scholars to provide is
not available.' Theologians, when seeking to formulate the doctrine of
the incarnation, have looked to the Gospels, not for the bare bones of
Jesus's biography, but for information about such subtle and intimate
matters as his so-called messianic consciousness, his moral perfection,
or his relationship with his Heavenly Father. So long as the divine
inspiration of the Bible was held to guarantee the literal truth of every
statement in it, such information may have seemed available: at most
it was a matter of inference from statements scattered about the
Gospels – and particularly in the Fourth Gospel – which seemed to
offer privileged insight into Jesus's nature and character. But the
results of modern criticism have made it impossible to use the evidence in this way. Anything which purports to be an answer to the
theologian's questions can be shown to be itself the product of
theological reflection in the early Church, and to offer no access to the
mind of Jesus himself. Treated as historical documents, as they now
must be, the Gospels can offer us secure information only of a factual
historical kind. To pursue such matters as a 'doctrine of the person of
Christ', the theologian will have to draw his conclusions from prem-

ises established elsewhere.

There is logic in this argument; but it is a logic that is cogent only so long as the theologian's task is conceived of in a certain way. If it is the case that Christology, for example, is a theological enterprise which consists in constructing a doctrinal edifice on the basis of certain propositions that can be found in the Bible concerning God, Jesus, and mankind, then the critical doubts to which this kind of statement about Jesus is now exposed will clearly prove fatal to the whole enterprise. Indeed, this appears to be precisely the conclusion reached by the authors of *The Myth of God Incarnate*. Direct evidence that Jesus was divine, they argue, can no longer be found in the New Testament; and here, I believe, they are quite correct: all the texts in which Jesus appears to be called 'God' are subject to textual or exegetical ambiguity. The conclusion is then drawn that since no propositions are available which would serve as a basis for the doctrine of the divinity of Christ, the whole enterprise must be abandoned and an altogether less exalted and exclusive category be found with which to describe him.

But is the task of theology correctly stated in this way? It is at least arguable that the traditional preoccupation of theology with propositional statements is one for which the Bible provides singularly inappropriate foundations. For the most part, the sense in which the Bible may be said to be true is not the same as that in which a proposition is true. The Bible is predominantly narrative, exhortation, poetry, prophecy. We may certainly say that these things are true; but we shall mean something different by 'truth' in each case. Theologians have traditionally been concerned with only one kind of truth: that which is possessed by propositions. But our argument is that there are, and always have been, other ways of speaking about God than by means of propositions, and that these other ways are equally susceptible of study by the disciplines of theology. Let me conclude this chapter by suggesting how this may be the case with regard to the theological assessment of the evidence about Jesus – that is, Christology.

We may begin with the obvious statement that the earliest Christians could hardly have occupied themselves with the question posed by later theologians: whether, and in what sense, Jesus was 'god'. The Jewish people were severely and passionately monotheist. That God is one, and that only he is God, was the foundation of their religion and their whole way of life, and was explicitly endorsed by Jesus himself. Therefore, among those Jews who were first converted to Christ, the idea could not have been entertained for one moment that Jesus was *another* god. Nor would it have occurred to them to think of Jesus as a manifestation of God on earth. The consequences of this would have been too horrifying to contemplate: for if, in the presence of Jesus, one had been in the presence of God himself, then the smallest failure to reverence and obey him, not only on the part of his enemies but also on the part of those who sought to follow him, would have been tantamount to blasphemy and punishable by instant death. Their notions of God were far too serious for them to envisage such a crude and merciless divine epiphany. On the other hand it was clear to them that Jesus was far more than just one more in the long succession of divinely authorized prophets, kings, and teachers who had figured in the history of Israel. There was, it seemed, a finality about him, a total authority, which made one's personal decision for or against him a matter of infinitely more moment than one's attention to or disregard of the words of any of God's previous messengers. How then was one to articulate this finality, this ultimate authority? One could use a number of titles, such as 'Christ' or 'Son of God', to convey the idea; but since a person such as Jesus had never been envisaged in Jewish religious thought, no term was available which could serve as short-hand for the claims these Christians had to make. They had no option but to do what in any case came more naturally to them than exact definitions of nature and status: to tell the story of Jesus in such a way that his unprecedented authority would become apparent and would confront their hearers, as it had confronted those who had witnessed it, with the necessity to make up their minds, to declare themselves for or against, to believe that Jesus was God's authorized agent, representative, and revealer on earth (for which such titles as Christ and Son of God could be made, in the context of the story, to serve), or to throw in their lot with those who, having rejected Jesus's claims, believed it to be their duty to put any such blasphemous impostor to death.

Seen in this light, the kind of information which I have argued is in fact available about Jesus from the Gospels no longer seems irrelevant to Christology. The task is not so much to define, in ontological terms, the exact relationship of the Son to his Heavenly Father – for which the New Testament offers little purchase – as to assess the evidence for the claim that Jesus spoke and acted in such a way that his authority could have proceeded only from God. For this task the narrative of the New Testament contains abundant materials for the theologian to consider. It yields impressive historical evidence that Jesus's style of teaching and action combined in an unprecedented way the roles of those who in earlier centuries had been acknowledged as God's authorized emissaries and teachers; he was believed to have brought about miraculous cures which were felt to be a foretaste of God's ultimate purposes for mankind; he spoke of the present moment as one which confronted every one of his hearers with a decisive choice; and he was condemned and executed as one who, though not clearly a transgressor of the Law himself, yet challenged everyone else's observance of it in a way that could not be tolerated by those responsible for its maintenance. By the narration of such episodes, and many more, the evangelists presented the case for acknowledging the authority of Jesus to have been and to be that of God himself, and challenged their readers to make their decision on the evidence. This is the very stuff of Christology, and is at least as accessible today as it ever has been. It is the task of the theologian to assess it, to articulate it, and to translate it into terms which will impose the same necessity of decision on all who are willing to attend to the Christian message today.

NOTES

1. *The Remaking of Christian Doctrine* (1975), p. 48.
2. Mark 5.1, according to the now generally accepted text.
3. Gadara, a town nearer the lake, but still too far from the shore to be appropriate (Matt. 8.28).
4. The MSS. of all three Synoptic Gospels offer the variants Gerasenes, Gadarenes, and Gergesenes (Gergesa being a place otherwise unknown).
5. Cf. D. E. Nineham, *The Use and Abuse of the Bible* (1976), *passim*, for an extreme statement of this view.
6. For an account, and sensible criticism, of this criterion, cf. R. S. Barbour, *Traditio-Historical Criticism of the Gospels* (1972), pp. 5ff.
7. The following paragraphs summarize an argument which will be substantiated in my forthcoming Bampton Lectures, *Jesus and the Constraints of History*, from which also several paragraphs of this chapter have been taken.

6

The Gospels without Christology

GEZA VERMES

'JESUS', as Julius Wellhausen pointed out in 1905 (and his statement still tends to shock), 'was not a Christian but a Jew.'[1] It was thought by my colleagues when this enterprise was being organized – and I hope that their example will be followed in future such debates – that the voice of a fellow-Jew, a lifelong student of first-century Palestine, would have the worthwhile effect of illuminating a face of Jesus perceptible only from outside the fold of the Church. But it must be stressed that although the tools used here derive from Jewish studies, the resulting work in no way constitutes an official Jewish stand on Christology. Judaism has no teaching on Jesus.

The immediate object of this essay is the problematic of Anthony Harvey's chapter, 'Christology and the Evidence of the New Testament'. Whether Christology is a suitable designation of 'a theological assessment of the evidence about Jesus' (p. 52) must be discussed later, but I am already on record as having expressed guarded optimism in regard to Harvey's basic contention that it is possible to discover what kind of an individual Jesus was. I have argued that an inquiry into the personality and doctrine of Jesus is viable provided that the Synoptic Gospels are subjected to a careful, sensitive, and enlightened historical scrutiny.[2] At the same time, it may be something of an exaggeration to maintain, as Harvey does, that only a 'few New Testament scholars of today would wish to say that we can have no reliable knowledge about Jesus' (p. 44).

As far as basic methodological assumptions are concerned, while agreement between our positions is far-reaching, several general questions unmentioned so far need to be raised, and some of the solutions proposed by him re-examined.

First, is it self-evident, as post-*Formgeschichte* New Testament specialists appear to think, that the composition of the Gospels is due entirely to the didactic-theological requirements of the primitive Church, and that they were never in any way intended to be 'historical'? If the evangelists were primarily resolved to teach Christian doctrine, was it not rather inept to adopt a biographical literary style, which provides liveliness and colour but at the expense of simplicity and clarity? Their story of Jesus is replete with Palestinian ideas,

customs, linguistic peculiarities, and *realia* of all sorts, incomprehens-
ible to non-Jewish readers and demanding continuous interpretative
digressions which were bound to be catechetically harmful. Furthermore, the evangelists preserve sayings of Jesus, and attitudes of mind,
actually in conflict with essential church teachings. For example, his
disparaging remarks about Gentiles, and his apparent unwillingness
to permit his followers to proclaim him Messiah, can hardly have
suited the requirements of the first promulgators of Christianity
trying to convince non-Jews that 'Jesus is the Christ' (John 20.31; cf.
Acts 2.36). Early teachers such as Paul, James, the author of Didache,
found in any case no advantage in 'biography' for the transmission of
theological expositions, moral exhortations, and disciplinary or litur-
gical rules, and opted sensibly for a direct method of communication.
It is therefore difficult to avoid concluding that the evangelists chose
to tell the life of Jesus because, whatever else they may have aimed at,
they were determined to recount history, however unprofessionally.
And if they include circumstances which were doctrinally embarras-
sing, it is because they genuinely form part of the narrative. In that
case, Bultmann's famous dictum to the effect that nothing can be
known of Jesus's story or personality 'because the early Christian
sources show no interest in either',[3] becomes a plain misjudgement.

In his quest for criteria of authenticity, Anthony Harvey and a
number of other New Testament scholars lend great importance to
the principle of 'dissimilarity'. While no one would deny that originality is significant, Harvey himself admits that today's oddity may turn
out to be tomorrow's commonplace, as has been amply shown by the
Qumran discoveries. Again, a feature found peculiar by one person
may not appear so to someone better informed.[4] And even those
'dissimilarities' which are not simply the result of ignorance may still
be no more than curiosities unless it can be proved that they are
consistent and form a coherent whole with the main themes of a
doctrine. But if sufficiently characteristic traits attested in a variety of
literary contexts (e.g., sayings, parables, narratives) and in more than
one source (e.g., Mark and Q) run through the entire gospel tradition
(like Jesus's attitude towards the outcasts of Jewish society), they
stand a good chance of constituting valid historical evidence.

Another element to be taken into account in a search for authenticity is the relative brevity of Jesus's career. Where the Gospels contain
contradictory teachings, they cannot be explained away as representing an evolution of Jesus's ideas. We cannot, that is, accept as genuine
Jesus's xenophobic utterances and surprise at apparent signs of faith
among non-Jews, *and* his institution of an apostolic mission to the
'nations', his foundation of an international 'catholic' Church.

Most importantly, also, no critical evaluation of the Gospels can
overlook the impact of Jesus's tragic fate on those who first chronicled

his story, and on the evangelists themselves. They present him as an envoy of God sent to usher in the Kingdom; yet, outside Galilee at least, his word went unheeded; he encountered nothing but hostility from the Judaean leaders; and he was finally brought before the Roman prefect and sentenced to die on a cross. He felt himself to have been abandoned by all, by God and by men. Could a person marked by such abysmal failure ever be accepted as ultimate spiritual master, as the elect of heaven, as Lord and Messiah? Unless the scandal of the crucifixion could be eliminated, the answer had to be no. And the historian cannot be blamed if, in those parts of Jesus's story which first imply, and subsequently argue, that the cross was divinely foreordained, he distinguishes the operations of early Christian apologists. He will apply the same judgement to the account of the resurrection, whereby disaster is turned into triumph, with a happy ending merely alluded to in the oldest Gospel but elaborated more and more fully by the later evangelists. On this topic, moreover, the Gospels display intrinsic contradictions. They assert on the one hand that Jesus repeatedly foretold his resurrection on the third day. On the other, they reveal the apostles in total disarray immediately after the crucifixion and quite unprepared for him to rise from the dead. Indeed, the Gospels themselves testify clearly to a progressive development, refinement, and reinforcement of the resurrection story. The first version is based on hearsay evidence brought by unreliable female witnesses. In the next, the news is confirmed by the trustworthy Peter and John. And subsequently, in a sort of first-hand testimony, apparitions of the risen Jesus are seen by an increasing number of disciples, culminating in a mass vision by over five hundred brethren, many of whom are said by Paul to be still alive – in distant Galilee? – at the time of his first letter to the Corinthians (1 Cor. 15.6).

Gospel references to the *parousia* have also to be placed within the setting of a career that ended in seeming ignominy. The resurrection argument is addressed only to believers; no outsider is recorded as having met the risen Jesus. The glorious second coming, by contrast, is to be his vindication before the whole world. In its earliest phase, this tradition expects the day of the Lord to be imminent, within the life-span of Jesus's own generation. But a decrescendo of apocalyptic fervour becomes perceptible in the New Testament itself. The members of the church in Thessalonica have to be advised to control their enthusiasm strictly; but only a little later, Christians are being encouraged to be watchful for the bridegroom may not arrive until midnight. And a little later still, they are being exhorted to cultivate the virtue of endurance. Finally, with the *parousia* still not realized, the apocalyptic momentum flags, and the *eschaton*, soon after the completion of the New Testament, is relegated to the distant future.

Here, therefore, is the dilemma confronting the critical student of the Gospels: either the *parousia* speculation was the outcome of Jesus's own notion of eschatology and apocalypticism, or it belongs to a separate domain. Either, that is to say, Jesus was himself responsible for promoting the expectation of his impending glorious return; or it has to be ascribed to Christian apologetics. In the first case, as will be explained, there would appear to be some incompatibility between such a role foreseen for himself and Jesus's essential religious outlook. In the second, however, strong support is provided by Qumran eschatology. In both Christianity and Essenism, the delay in the coming of the Lord's day is attended by exhortations to courage and patience. 'The final age shall be prolonged', reads the Habakkuk Commentary, 'and shall exceed all that the Prophets have said; for the mysteries of God are astounding. *If it tarries, wait for it, for it shall surely come and shall not be late* (Hab. 2.3). Interpreted, this concerns the men of truth who keep the Law, whose hands shall not slacken in the service of truth when the final age is prolonged. For all the ages of God reach their appointed end as He determines for them in the mysteries of His wisdom' (vii.7–14).

The purpose of these methodological remarks must by now be obvious. If we accept that in recounting the life of Jesus the motive of the evangelists was, to some extent at least, to write history, and if it seems a reasonable probability that the resurrection and *parousia* material should be attributed to the doctrinal and apologetic needs of the early Church, it becomes as clear *a posteriori* as it has been *a priori* that our understanding of the real Jesus must derive basically from an analysis of the synoptic data concerning his life and teaching that is unaffected by accretions springing from the creative imagination of nascent Christianity.

No particular novelty distinguishes the portrait of Jesus which follows. For that matter, in a field so thoroughly turned and re-turned over the centuries, any truly revolutionary theory could not but be suspect. But it is still possible, by telling a familiar story from an unusual angle, to open up new approaches to the whole ancient problem.

The New Testament presentation of the 'Christ-event', still embryonic in the Synoptic Gospels, though fully developed in the Pauline writings, seeks to proclaim the salvific function of the suffering, death, and resurrection of Jesus. The ordinary details of his life and teaching receive only secondary attention compared with the stress laid on the ultimate purpose of his mission, and are viewed from the central stand of theology. In fact, it is sometimes held that since the 'dogmatic' approach to the story dominates at every level of its transmission, it is unscholarly to discard it and to try to peer behind the screen of the primitive Christian 'myth'. Anyway, is it likely that Jesus's early followers misrepresent most of the major issues, and that the historian of today, after the lapse of nineteen centuries, can make good their mistakes and trace a more reliable image of the happenings of their time?

On the face of it, it certainly appears improbable. But it is not impossible and methodologically not illegitimate. First, in spite of all the redactional and editorial manipulation introduced by the individual evangelists and by the primitive Church, we can still detect in the Synoptic Gospels the outline of a portrait of Jesus which, as has been already noted, departs radically from the figure drawn on the theological canvas of Paul. A concrete basis therefore exists on which to situate a historical reconstruction. Second, the critical student of the Gospels must bear in mind the cataclysms which took place in the earliest stages of the formation of Christianity. The culture to which Jesus belonged was Jewish, Palestinian-Galilean , Aramaic-Hebrew, whereas from the middle of the first century onwards, Christianity grew mostly on Graeco-Roman soil, in a Graeco-Hellenistic civilization.[5] So although in one sense there was continuity, in another there was a major uprooting so profound as to rule out Gentile Christianity as a reliable source for an historical understanding of Jesus the Jew. In many respects, the Hebrew Bible and post-biblical Judaism are better equipped to illuminate the original significance of words and deeds recorded in the Gospels. Finally, we have to ask ourselves, why the earliest Jewish followers of Jesus withdrew from the mainstream of the Christian movement. The problem concerns us here because it is logical to suppose that one reason may have been that they felt that Jesus's original ideals were being abandoned and replaced by alien concepts and aspirations.

These preliminaries bring us at last to the Synoptic Gospels and our search for the 'real' Jesus. In an earlier publication I have argued that those who witnessed the major part of his public life, namely, his Galilean contemporaries, regarded him as a healer and exorcist, a magnetic teacher and holy man.[6] Anthony Harvey agrees with this assessment and lists both functions among the 'statements about Jesus which are known with as much certainty as is the case with any notable figure of the ancient world' (p.48). But our views overlap only in part and further investigation is called for. He surely goes too far in describing Jesus's charismatic acts as 'for the most part without precedent in his own culture' (p.49). The existence of literary parallels is incontestable. Exegetical scholarship has been acquainted for some time with stories relating to Hanina ben Dosa, and more recently I have tried to show that when presented critically, they are more relevant than New Testament interpreters are inclined to admit.[7] It is equally obvious that emphasis on miraculous activities is a legacy of prophetic religion as manifested in the lives of Elijah and Elisha, a type of popular piety preserved throughout the centuries, where the hero is the 'man of God' rather than the priest or sage.[8] In an age when the combination of sanctity and the miraculous was considered normal, Jesus would have been an outstanding representative of holiness. Contemporary Jewish authorities frowned on charismatic practices as potential or actual threats to orderly life, but usually they could do little about them because of the high esteem in which wonder-workers were generally held. Rabbinic thought itself is ambivalent in regard to the miraculous. The appearance of such phenomena in the Bible and in post-biblical times is taken for granted by the masters of Mishnah, Talmud, and Midrash, as well as by the Targumists; though they often suggest that their own generation, not so eager for martyrdom, is no longer worthy of miracles (Babylonian Talmud: Berakhoth 20a). But the large number of *obiter dicta* indicates that the idea of the miracle remained common currency in spite of the rabbis and their attempts to reduce the value of the supernatural. A miracle is said to be inferior to rational argument in academic debate (Babylonian Talmud: Bava Metsica 59b); and a non-miraculous cure from fever (described as heavenly fire) is ranked higher than the 'miraculous' deliverance of the three youths from the fiery furnace, the flames of which were natural and could have been extinguished with water (Babylonian Talmud: Nedarim 41a).

That Jesus was in addition a renowned exorcist is well attested. Inheriting the inter-Testamental vision of a world ruled by spirits of light and darkness, he rejected the notion that the struggle against darkness was the sole business of a heavenly army to which humans could offer no more than insignificant assistance. He democratized the whole conception of the fight against the devil. At a time when nervous and mental disorders were attributed to demonic possession, he healed minds by getting the better of the evil spirits inhabiting them. And he mended the sick bodies of men and women convinced that their illness was the result of sin by loosing Satan's grip on them through forgiveness of the offences thought to be the cause of their disease. The same ideology survives even in a Talmudic saying: 'No sick man shall recover from his illness until all his sins have been pardoned' (bNed. 41a).

Besides ministering as healer and exorcist, Jesus certainly taught. But is Anthony Harvey correct in describing him as an expert in the Law and in the technicalities of Jewish Bible interpretation? On the whole, the picture of Jesus that he sees emerging from the Gospels in this particular respect is that of a learned rabbi involved in scholarly controversy with 'authorized exponents' of the Torah. It would of course be more than injudicious to reject out of hand the definition of biblical expert, for after all a number of the arguments mentioned between Jesus and others turn on points of Scripture interpretation. Nevertheless, our knowledge – admittedly imperfect – of Galilean culture of the late Second Temple era, and the New Testament evidence itself provide a certain measure of support for the opinion that Jesus was an amateur in the field. In the first instance, expert Bible exegesis was normally the prerogative of the Pharisees; yet neither Josephus, nor rabbinic literature, indicate any noticeable Pharisee presence or Pharisee doctrinal impact in the northern province prior to A.D. 70, or even 135.[9] In addition, there is no hint in the Gospels that Jesus received any kind of religious training of this sort, not to speak of the fact that Galileans were in general not conspicuous for their erudition. But in any case, the bulk of the literary forms in which Jesus's special teaching is expressed (wisdom sayings, prophetic warnings, parables, etc.) demand no peculiar skill in exegesis proper. Indeed, all three synoptists specify at the outset of Jesus's preaching career that his style differed from that of the rabbis. He taught with 'authority' and *not* like the scribes (Mark 1.22 and par.), whose prime concern was to present all religious doctrine as sanctioned by tradition and originating in Scripture. In view of these considerations, the proposals of the form-critics to postdate many of the scholastic discussions and controversies between Jesus and the Pharisees and identify them as exchanges between Palestinian church leaders and their 'rabbinic' opponents, acquire particular cogency. Jesus was a charismatic healer, but also a charismatic teacher, whose words possessed great power, convincing those who heard them that they were listening to a man of God.

Anthony Harvey's further assertion that the contemporaries of Jesus 'must . . . have discerned in him those attributes which belonged to the traditional idea of prophet' (p.47) is safe enough. But how does he define 'prophet'? He writes: 'The essence of the prophet is that he relates his message to a specific moment in history and invests the moment in which he delivers it with particular significance' (pp.49–50). This definition may correspond to the modern view of prophecy, but no Jew living in the inter-Testamental age is likely to have thought along such lines. From the testimony of post-biblical Judaism and of the Gospels themselves, it is clear that at that time two notions of prophecy prevailed, one scholarly and the other popular. For the scholar, a prophet was one believed to be endowed with supernatural foresight and discernment ('If this man were a prophet, he would have known who and what sort of woman this is who is touching him' [Luke 7.39]). For the people, however, the prophet was a powerful spokesman and mediator, and often a miracle-worker ('A prophet mighty in deed and word before God and all the people' [Luke 24.19]). Jesus will have been recognized as a prophet by his disciples in either or both of these senses. Would he himself have replied in the affirmative to the question, 'Are you a prophet'? Possibly. Though on balance, it is easier to imagine him avoiding a straight answer. His single-minded absorption was in his mission and task, not in the role he was playing. It is doubtful, in consequence, whether there is much justification for Harvey's reference to 'constraints imposed by this role of a prophet', within which Jesus 'must have been conditioned and prepared to act' (p.47).

This mention of titles and roles brings us face to face with the real crux inherent in any historical estimate of the figure of Jesus. The religious outlook of Christianity, from Paul onwards, has always been *christocentric*. In the faith of the Church, the crucified and risen Lord is Messiah, Saviour, Son of God, and finally God proper. Belief that his death and resurrection have the power to atone for the sins of the world and redeem it, is of the essence of Christianity. But did Jesus think in these terms? Were they part of his own religion?

It is no good turning to Paul for enlightenment, since he never in his life set eyes on Jesus. Paul's 'gospel' sprang from a mystical revelation of his own, mingled with a smattering of knowledge obtained at second hand. As a witness to Jesus's personal thinking, sentiments, and spiritual perspective he is simply unqualified.

Jesus, as I have said apropos of the role of prophet, and as is more than obvious from even the most cursory reading of the Gospels, was without any shadow of doubt entirely unself-centred. His piety was unreservedly *theocentric*. 'Why do you call me good? No one is good but God alone' (Mark 10.18) – this is a rejection by him of an excess of enthusiasm for his person on the part of his admirers. His destiny as he saw it was purely to guide them along the way towards the Kingdom of Heaven, towards submission to the sovereignty of God.

Anthony Harvey is not in disagreement with this. '(Jesus's) evident concern for the reign of God,' he writes, 'almost to the exclusion of discussion of his own status and destiny, remains an important piece of unimpeachable information about him' (p.50). But to appreciate the significance of this statement, we need to see in sharper focus the religion which Jesus preached and practised. Only by coming closer to an approximation of Jesus's own authentic teaching can we properly appraise the Christology of the Church.

He was no philosopher. Speculations *in abstracto* on the nature of God and on the divine mysteries were of no moment to him. God was for him no transcendent idea or *ens per se*. For him, God was invested with the two traditional forms of King and Father. It is not certain that the synagogal prayer *avinu malkenu*, 'Our Father our King', existed already in the first decades of the Christian era (the Talmud ascribes it to Rabbi Akiva in the early second century [Babylonian Talmud: Taᶜanith 25b]), but there can be little doubt that these two concepts of the Deity were widely current in Jesus's time.

That the theme of the sovereignty of God is basic to Jesus's teaching is beyond question. On the other hand, it should be pointed out that the notions of 'King' and 'Kingdom' are not to be pressed too hard. It would be a mistake always to look for strictly 'royal' associations or – worse still – for further associations with royal Messianism and heavenly enthronement. Kingdom parables exist in which the chief actor is a monarch; but they are few. Jesus's tendency to democratize, alluded to already in connection with the conflict between light and darkness, is apparent in relation to the Kingdom also. In a Talmudic parable, it is a king who hires workers for his vineyard (Palestinian Talmud: Berakhoth ii, 5c); in the Gospel (Matt. 20.1), it is a householder. But the really idiosyncratic feature of Jesus's representation of the Kingdom is the frequent absence from it of any royal paraphernalia such as thrones, chariots, armies, courtiers, choirs, etc. He uses instead similes borrowed from the rustic and domestic life of Galilean peasants and from the affairs of fishermen. The Kingdom of Heaven resembles the field, the seed and the sower, the vineyard, the mustard plant and the fig-tree, the fish, the net and the catch, the poor woman looking for the lost *drachma*, the leaven and the dough. In the most characteristic of the Gospel examples, the Kingdom is not an apocalyptic, spectacular, future reality. It belongs to the here and now. It is of immediate concern to all while it grows and develops imperceptibly, in quiet mystery. Only Jesus's acts of healing and exorcism provide a faint glimpse of its presence. 'But if it is by the finger [or the Spirit] of God that I cast out demons, then the kingdom of God has come upon you' (Luke 11.20; Matt. 12.28).

When Jesus declares that the Kingdom is in the midst of his generation, he is alluding to those who, heeding his prophetic appeal, and that of the Baptist before him, have turned to God and made their *teshuvah* (conversion). But for him, 'Thy kingdom come' equals 'Thy will be done' (Matt. 6.10). The Kingdom will come by way of obedience to 'the Law and the Prophets', summarized in the decalogue (Mark 10.17–23 and par.) and quintessentially represented in the great commandment of love (Mark 12.28–34 and par.). And while he lays extraordinary emphasis on the inner, moral, and religious significance of the Law, it is not he, the Galilean Jesus, who excuses its non-performance. It is the Diaspora Hellenist, Paul, who proclaims it to be non-binding. Jesus, in fact, exhorts the people to observe the ritual precepts of the Torah. He orders the lepers whom he has cured to report to the priests and to undergo the ceremony prescribed by Moses. He explicitly approves of the sending of gifts to the Temple (Matt. 5.23) and of the commandment of tithing (which was probably not very popular among the farmers of his region) [cf. Mark 1.44 and par.; Luke 17.14; Matt. 23.23; Luke 11.42]. He is even depicted as recommending the whole pharisaic legal teaching or *halakhah* (Matt.

23.2–3). The only exceptions, more apparent than real, have to do with discrepancies in interpreting certain legal customs, or with the conflict between one law and another, such as the law of Sabbath rest and that of saving life (Matt. 12.11; Luke 14.5).

Equal in importance to the Kingdom motif in Jesus's teaching is that of his status as son of his Father in heaven, a relationship which he insists repeatedly is not exclusive to himself but attainable by all. Addressing God as 'Abba', he teaches his disciples to do the same, or to use, when praying, the more solemn invocation, 'Our Father who art in heaven'. This style, as has been already suggested, is one of the peculiarities of Hasidic prayer in ancient Judaism. According to the Mishnah, 'the Hasidim of old spent an hour (in recollection) in order to direct their hearts towards their Father in heaven' (Mishnah: Berakhoth 5.1). And again, 'Since the destruction of the Temple', asked the second-century holy man, Pinhas ben Yair, 'on whom can we rely? On our Father who is in heaven' (Babylonian Talmud: Sotah 49a; cf. Mishnah: Sotah 9.15 with the same saying attributed to Rabbi Eliezer the Great). Again, in an anecdote relating to Abba Hanan, a first-century B.C. miracle-worker, he was pursued during a drought by children shouting: 'Abba, Abba, give us rain!' His response was to entreat the 'Lord of the Universe' to 'render service to those who cannot distinguish between the Abba who gives rain and the Abba who does not' (Babylonian Talmud: Ta῾annith 23b).

Whether genuine or not, the celebrated words of thanksgiving placed in the mouth of Jesus by the evangelists express with great perspicuity his ideal of reciprocity between Father and son. 'All things have been delivered to me by my Father; and no one knows who the son is except the Father, or who the Father is except the son and any one to whom the son chooses to reveal him' (Luke 10.22; Matt. 11.27). Reciprocity is, however, not equality, and it is remarkable that even in sayings actually traceable to the primitive Church and not to Jesus, the Father's superiority remains impregnable. The 'son' does not know the hour of the end (Mark 13.32; Matt. 24.36) or possess authority to allocate places in the Kingdom (Mark 10.40; Matt. 20.23). Both are privileges belonging to the Father alone. Paul lends his voice to support the same order of precedence, foretelling that in the apocalyptic triumph the 'son' shall be subject to God (1 Cor. 15.28).

These apparently theoretical statements about God must not mislead us: they are, as has been suggested, probably formulations composed by the Church. Jesus's own message, on this as on all other topics, is genuinely existential. He has in mind behaviour rather than theory, a lived relation of son with the Father rather than a determination of his spiritual pedigree. When he points to the child as the best example of true piety, he sees in a child's total simplicity and trust a paradigm of the biblical virtue of faith or *emunah*. His words speak for themselves. 'Ask, and it will be given you; seek, and you will find; knock, and it will be opened to you. For every one who asks receives, and he who seeks finds, and to him who knocks it will be opened. Or what man of you, if his son asks him for a loaf, will give him a stone? Or if he asks for a fish, will give him a serpent? If you then, who are evil, know how to give good gifts to your children, how much more will your Father who is in heaven give good things to those who ask him?' (Matt. 7.7–11; Luke 11.9–13).

Jesus goes even further. He dares to advise his disciples to adopt the attitude not only of children but of spoilt children, to importune their Heavenly Father until he grants their request. This may again be seen as pointing to Jesus's Hasidic inheritance. Honi's petulant challenge that he would not cross the circle which he had drawn around himself until God showed mercy towards his sons, provoked the resentful comment from Simeon ben Shetah, the Pharisee leader: 'If you were not Honi, I would excommunicate you. But what can I do with you, since even though you pester God, he does what you wish, in the same way that a father does what his persistent son asks him?' (Mishnah: Taʿannith 3.8). The rabbis, stressing always the need for correct behaviour, disapprove of such temerity, though they admit that sometimes it works. 'Impertinence (*hutspa*) has its usefulness even towards heaven' (Babylonian Talmud: Sanhedrin 105a)!

It should be noted in connection with the Father-Son relationship that in Jesus's religious message the worship of God is inseparable from responsible action towards the world. Love of God and love of one's fellow jointly constitute the first commandment. Blessings and gifts received from the Heavenly Father must serve as models for the children in their conduct towards one another. The commandment to love one's enemies sees this doctrine formulated in its most exaggerated form, for it is the enemy who provides the ideal opportunity for the good deed without expectation of return. 'Love your enemies . . . so that you may be sons of your Father who is in heaven; for he makes his sun rise on the evil and on the good, and sends rain on the just and on the unjust' (Matt. 5.44–5; cf. Luke 6.32–5).

Jesus's recognition of himself as son of God, and his encouragement to others to develop the same self-awareness in their position *vis-à-vis* God, entailed putting into effect Judaism's foremost religious principle: the *imitatio dei*. As Targum and Midrash insist, those who strive for holiness must 'walk in God's ways'. 'As he is merciful and gracious, you must also be merciful and gracious' (Mekhilta on Exod. 15.2). 'As the Holy One is called righteous . . . so you also must be righteous; as the Holy One is called *hasid*, you also must be *hasid*' (Sifre on Deut. 49). 'My people, children of Israel, as your Father is merciful in heaven, so must you also be merciful on earth' (Targum

Ps. –Jonathan on Lev. 22.28). Jesus's instruction is the same. 'Be merciful, even as your Father is merciful.' 'You, therefore, must be perfect, as your heavenly Father is perfect' (Luke 6.36; Matt. 5.48). But also, in his care and love for sinners and outcasts, Jesus displays another aspect of *imitatio*: imitating the Father, he takes up the role of father himself towards those who need his comfort and help and expects his disciples to do the same.

This concept of a filial relation with God is inseparable in Jesus's thinking from the eschatologico-apocalyptic mentality typical of first-century Judaism, and the combination of the two may account for his total lack of concern for the economic and political realities of contemporary existence. Recent attempts to transform him into a social or nationalistic revolutionary not only find no confirmation in the Gospels but appear irreconcilable with his particular type of piety. If he is convinced that the Father provides for his children, he has to show that material preoccupations and careful planning for the future are contrary to true religion. 'Do not be anxious about your life, what you shall eat or what you shall drink, nor about your body, what you shall put on . . . Look at the birds of the air . . . Consider the lilies of the field. . . .' (Matt. 6.25–8; Luke 12.22–7). 'Are not two sparrows sold for a penny? And not one of them will fall to the ground without your Father's will. But even the hairs of your head are all numbered. Fear not, therefore; you are of more value than many sparrows' (Matt. 10.29–31; cf. Luke 12.6–7). Earthly riches are perishable; thieves can steal them, moth and rust devour them (Matt. 6.19–21; Luke 12.33–4). The best devised plans can and often do misfire (Luke 12.14–21). What matters is not tomorrow or next year, but today. It is the present time that is endowed with unique, and therefore infinite, importance. 'Do not be anxious about tomorrow. . . . Let the day's own trouble be sufficient for the day' (Matt. 6.34).

By comparison, when Jesus considers the affairs of the Kingdom, all is extreme urgency. The teacher is to be followed at once. The disciple's father must be buried by someone else (Matt. 8.22; Luke 9.60). The field with the hidden treasure, the precious pearl unrecognized by others, must be gained at whatever cost, without delay (Matt. 13.44–6).

It should be added in parenthesis that this exclusive concentration on the eschatological here and now leaves no room whatever for a distant future. It represents in consequence a religious vision incompatible with the institution of an organized hierarchic body expected to endure. If it reflects Jesus's own thinking, he cannot be made responsible for the foundation of the Church. It was the extinction of the *parousia* hope, cultivated in self-contained Christian communities, that conferred permanent status on a structure which was originally not expected to endure beyond a brief span.

Can the message of Jesus be summarized in any meaningful way? Motivated by a central vision of God as King and Father, the main purpose of his short existence was to give reality to his own filial relation by living as a son of God, and to show to the repentant and the receptive how to live similarly. His understanding of his own obligations, and those of his followers, combined with the pressures of the eschatologico-apocalyptic world-view which they had all inherited, conferred a quality of urgency and uncompromising self-surrender on his entire religious action. It is this single-minded, unreserved, enthusiastic piety, this unceasing struggle to reproduce in himself, in his dealings with the world, the attributes of his Heavenly Father, that strikes the historian as Jesus's unique contribution to the history of religion, one which as a source of inspiration and model of holiness possesses a real, timeless, and universal significance and appeal. They are also the qualities that so overwhelmed the apostles and disciples that even the collapse of Jesus's ministry was unable to extinguish the faith which he had kindled in them.

How by comparison does Christology appear to the detached observer? It is, to begin with, a highly equivocal term, with at least three meanings. Etymologically, Christology and Messianism are synonymous, so in traditional Christian theological usage the word itself prejudges two major historical issues. It implies both that Jesus was aware of his messianic role, and that his destiny was the fulfilment of Jewish messianic expectation. Neither of these assumptions can be taken for granted. Careful consideration of the gospel data indicates that he may have been unzealous about being proclaimed Messiah for the simple reason that, since he did not comply with the essential requisites of the common messianic hope of Judaism, he did not feel the title applied to him.[10]

However, New Testament scholars advance a second definition of Christology–Messianism, one that adds to the normal concept of a saintly and valorous royal saviour various and varied messianic notions deriving from all sorts of circles, at different times, and held by many, or only a few, or even by a single individual. Presumed to be Jewish Messianism in the age of Jesus as distinct from the primitive royal idea, these notions provide ample scope for detecting features which match up to Jesus the Christ.

Proof of Jesus's messianic dignity is needed only in order to confirm that the biblical promises were fulfilled in him, that he was the one who was to come. But theology can dispense quite easily with such a historical requirement; Jesus's status is part of its faith and demands no demonstration.

This leads to the third sense of Christology as an umbrella notion covering reflection on all the New Testament data relative to Jesus. Assemble everything that contributes to belief in Christ and you have

Christology. The business of a 'Christologist' unaffected by historical considerations is not to ask if the points in question (e.g., the titles Lord, son of Man, son of God, etc.) are susceptible to non-dogmatic interpretation. He is not concerned with the real Jesus, but with expounding, and if necessary superimposing on the Gospel, the a-temporal, meta-historical 'Christ myth' of incarnation–atonement–redemption formulated and reformulated following the changing intellectual fashions of the ages.

Serious complications arise when New Testament specialists sensitive to history endeavour to pursue both disciplines simultaneously and apply the tools of the historian to the theologian's inquiry. They arrive at a historical conclusion – for example, that Jesus was a prophet – but find themselves immediately impelled to work their way back to their own theological territory where he becomes a prophet endowed with 'finality' and 'ultimate authority' (p.53). They concede that, when read critically, the New Testament offers no evidence that Jesus was God or 'a manifestation of God on earth' (p.52) – but at once go on to detect in the Gospels a 'case for acknowledging the authority of Jesus to have been and to be that of God himself' (p.54).

In attempting to combine two incompatibles, has theology, the historian wonders, involved itself in an enterprise by definition impossible?[11]

NOTES

1. *Einleitung in die drei ersten Evangelien* (1905), p. 113.
2. See my *Jesus the Jew – A Historian's Reading of the Gospels* (1973), p. 42 and p. 235, note 1.
3. Jesus and the Word, E.T. (1958), p.14.
4. Thus those who rely exclusively on Strack and Billerbeck for information relating to the rabbinic background material in the Gospels may deduce, from an absence of parallels in the *Kommentar*, an originality on the part of Jesus which did not exist. The silence may be due purely to an oversight by Billerbeck, or to his under-utilization of certain categories of Jewish writings, such as the Targums.
5. *Jesus the Jew*, pp. 83–4.
6. Ibid., pp. 22–9.
7. Ibid., pp. 72–8.
8. See J. B. Segal, 'Popular Religion in Ancient Israel', *Journal of Jewish Studies*, 27 (1976), pp. 7–9, 20–1.
9. *Jesus the Jew*, pp. 42–57.
10. Ibid., pp. 129–59.
11. For a fuller discussion of these questions see my Riddell Memorial Lectures, *The Gospel of Jesus the Jew*, to be published shortly by the University of Newcastle upon Tyne.

7

The Concept of a Christ-Event

JOHN MACQUARRIE

MY purpose is to explore what is meant by the expression 'Christ-event' as used by some recent theologians and New Testament scholars, and to ask further whether it is helpful or even legitimate to make the Christ-event rather than Jesus Christ himself the central topic of christological discussion.

On the second of these points, it might be objected that the expression 'Jesus Christ' is one with a definite referend, namely, a human individual who suffered under Pontius Pilate and who, whether intentionally or not, became the founder of the Christian religion; whereas the expression 'Christ-event' is a very fuzzy one. It is a somewhat odd and unnatural expression, presumably introduced into English as a translation of the German *Christusereignis*. It is used in a variety of senses, and while its range of reference is sometimes narrowed to the events which initiated Christianity, it can also be expanded to become almost coterminous with the whole of Christian history with perhaps Old Testament history thrown in as well for good measure. The word 'event' is ordinarily used for a much more limited type of happening than the complex that can be brought under the umbrella of Christ-event. So the suspicion is bound to arise that this habit of talking of the Christ-event may be a theological mystification designed to evade difficult questions about the individual, Jesus Christ.

But perhaps this objection rests on the mistake of supposing that the expression 'Jesus Christ' is more straightforward than it really is. It looks like a proper name, and indeed it is used as a proper name. I have even seen it listed in an index under the letter C as 'Christ, Jesus'! But logicians have been agreed for a long time that although proper names are primarily denotative, they also have a descriptive element. I may remind the reader of Bertrand Russell's much-discussed essay, 'Knowledge by Acquaintance and Knowledge by Description'.[1] There are two ways in which we can know a person. We can know him by acquaintance, through having met him. For instance, if I ask, 'Do you know Edward Jones?' you might reply, 'Yes, I met him at a party last week.' I might go on to say, 'Do you know that he is Professor of Animal Pathology at St Swithun's University?' Here I would be offering a description. You might reply, 'No, I didn't know, but now you mention it, it explains some of the conversation I had with him last week.' But even before you were given this description, the expression 'Edward Jones' was not purely demonstrative. You already thought of him as 'the person I met at a party'. Any particular, whether a thing or a person, cannot be known in pure isolation. A mere knowledge by acquaintance could consist only in pointing to the particular and saying 'This!' But we always place particulars in contexts and describe them by means of universals. Ordinary proper names resemble both demonstrative symbols ('This!') and descriptive phrases ('whom I met at a party'). Susan Stebbing has pointed out that 'the Greek use of the definite article *ho* before an ordinary proper name brings out very well this double significance; thus *ho Sokrates* stands for "the individual who has been introduced by the name Socrates" '.[2]

These remarks on acquaintance, description, and proper names will have made it clear that when we use a proper name, then simply on grounds of logic and epistemology, the referend of that name is not an isolated particular but is already linked with a descriptive context, and this may be more or less extensive and presumably more or less important. In the case of Jesus Christ, this context extends on the one side into the history and traditions of Israel, on the other into the primitive Church and the Hellenistic world. So the referend of the expression 'Jesus Christ' may not be so obvious as it seemed at first sight, and the notion of a Christ-event may be not so much a mystification as an attempt to draw attention to the penumbra that surrounds any proper name and that may turn out to have a special significance in the case of Jesus Christ.

The case of Jesus Christ is in fact rather special, or, at least, unusual, because the expression 'Christ', which already in the Pauline epistles is beginning to be treated as part of a proper name, was, as is generally supposed, originally a descriptive phrase that had been attached to the proper name 'Jesus', so that 'Jesus Christ' is originally 'Jesus the Christ'. The word 'Christ' presumably tended to lose its descriptive force – and this would happen especially among Gentile Christians – and to become primarily demonstrative. Yet the matter was even more complicated, for, on the other hand, the name 'Jesus' could, for those who were cognizant of its etymology, acquire the descriptive significance of 'he who saves', and was in fact understood by some in this way (Matt.1.21). Again, as the word 'Christ' was faltering in its descriptive function, new descriptions were brought along to interpret it. The confession 'You are the Christ' (Mark 8.29) became enlarged to 'You are the Christ, the Son of the living God' (Matt.16.16), and presumably this new description not only elucidates the older one, but introduces further nuances, and, beyond that, invites further interpretations in what could be a never-ending process.

It is clear that the various descriptive phrases I have quoted as applied to Jesus also imply certain propositions. Interestingly, some of these propositions correspond in form very closely with propositions which Russell used to illustrate his theory of descriptions, and we may find it useful to consider how he went about analysing such propositions. I choose three propositions that include christological descriptions:

1. 'Jesus is the Christ.'
2. 'The Christ is the Son of the living God.'
3. 'Jesus is (both) the Christ (and) the Son of the living God.'

With these we may compare the three following propositions from Russell:

1. 'Scott is the author of *Waverley*.'
2. 'The author of *Waverley* is the author of *Marmion*.'
3. 'Scott is the author of both *Waverley* and *Marmion*.'

According to Russell, the first of his three propositions is not the simple elementary proposition that it seems to be, but is itself equivalent to the conjoint assertion of three propositions:

i. 'At least one person wrote *Waverley*.'
ii. 'At most one person wrote *Waverley*.'
iii. 'There is nobody who both wrote *Waverley* and is not identical with Scott.'

So the proposition would be false if no one had written *Waverley*, or if more than one person had written it, or if some person other than Scott had written it. This analysis begins to let us see the complexities of the assertion, 'Jesus is the Christ', and not least the unspoken assumptions entailed by this apparently straightforward claim. If the claim is true, then it would need to be true that there exists (or has existed) someone who is 'the Christ' (an expression that obviously calls for much elucidation), that there is (or has been) only one such person, and that this person is none other than Jesus of Nazareth.

In the case of Russell's second proposition, 'The author of *Waverley* is the author of *Marmion*', nothing at all is said about Scott. We are bringing together two descriptions, and saying that if one of them applies, the other applies also. But the two descriptions are not identical. Being the author of *Marmion* adds something to being the author of *Waverley* – for instance, it adds the property of being a poet to that of being a novelist. Going back to our theological example, 'The Christ is the Son of the living God', there is here no mention of Jesus, but there is a conjunction of descriptions. We are specifying more fully what is meant by 'the Christ', and since the proposition is concerned with descriptions, or images, or concepts, it might be true even if Jesus were not the Christ or indeed if no one were the Christ. Although in fact the descriptions have been applied to Jesus, it is logically possible that they could be applied to someone else or even that there is no one to whom they apply. The analysis reveals that there are at least two distinct tasks in Christology. One is the exploration of christological images and concepts and the relations among them – Christ, Son of God, God-man, and so on. The other is their application to Jesus of Nazareth. It would be tempting to say that the first of these tasks is speculative, the second historical, but this would be oversimplifying the matter. Obviously the first of the tasks also raises historical questions, about the origin and development of such a description as 'the Christ', while the application of the description to Jesus raises questions that are not simply historical.

The third proposition in both sets can be derived from the other two. It applies the new enlarged description to the subject who, it is claimed, instantiates it. Clearly this could be the beginning of a process in which the description gets more and more elaborated. 'Ultimately,' according to Walter Kasper, 'Christology is no more than the exposition of the confession that Jesus is the Christ.'[3] Edward Schillebeeckx tries to reach a stratum earlier than the Christ and holds that 'the eschatological prophet' is 'the matrix of all the other honorific titles and credal strands'.[4] It does not much matter exactly where we begin – the point is that when one uses the expression 'Jesus Christ', its referend is the whole complex of descriptions that have been unpacked and applied to Jesus, and it is this complex of Jesus and his context that some recent theologians have designated by the shorthand expression, 'the Christ-event'.

Two difficult questions arise out of the foregoing discussion. Do we know Jesus Christ only by description and not at all by acquaintance? And, are the descriptions that have been applied to Jesus Christ logically comparable to the descriptions we find in Russell?

The first of these questions may seem a strange one. No one now living has been acquainted with Jesus Christ, in the way we ordinarily use the expression. We do not know him in the way that we know the man whom we met at a party last week. On the other hand, Christians have claimed from the beginning that Christ rose from the dead and is alive and present in his Church. Preachers and theologians have been telling us for centuries that we should know Christ at first hand rather than at second hand. Many Christians have in fact claimed to have had visions of Christ or encounters with Christ or to have known the presence of Christ in some more general way. I do not discount these claims, but their appeal is to a type of experience so different from what Russell had in mind that I think it might be confusing to say that they are instances of 'knowledge by acquaintance'.

There is another possibility. In the Gospels there are preserved in at least some instances the actual words of Jesus, so that when we read these words or hear them read in public worship, we come into a relationship which might, without straining the expression too far, be called 'acquaintance'. Hans Küng, in rather similar fashion, has ventured to speak of the 'audibility' of Jesus, and has claimed that 'through the transmitted word, a historical person can make himself heard even over the span of the centuries'.[5] The claim, of course, need not be confined to Jesus. One might say that while knowing that Scott is the author of *Waverley* is to know him by description, an actual reading of *Waverley* provides something like a direct encounter with Scott himself, though he has been dead for a century and a half. It may be that Russell has not drawn the distinction between knowledge by acquaintance and knowledge by description with sufficient care, or, again, that his analysis is at fault and the disjunction between these two ways of knowing is not exhaustive, so that there are intermediate possibilities. If all our knowledge of those who had died before our time were knowledge by description, would there be any way of testing the truth of the descriptions? Does there not remain some residual knowledge by acquaintance, transmitted in various ways?

The second question asks about the difference between two types of description, represented by the expressions 'the author of *Waverley*', and 'the Christ'. The first of these descriptions is factual and historical, and since there are extant today many copies of *Waverley*, we cannot doubt that someone must have written it. We can also imagine ways in which we might check whether Scott was the author, for instance, searching out letters between Scott and his publishers. But 'the Christ' is not a factual description of the same kind; rather, an evaluating and possibly also ontological description, offered from the point of view of a faith nurtured in a certain tradition. It would be open to someone to say that there is no one to whom the description 'the Christ', applies. We cannot here go into the large question of the nature and validity of the language of faith,[6] but having noted that there is this important difference between the two types of descriptive phrase, we should notice that there is also an important measure of similarity. Both Scott and Jesus are described not in terms of any personal characteristics but in terms of a wider 'event' in which each of them has a central place. We do not describe them by tracing their ancestries or giving information about the colour of their eyes or the like. That information is available in the case of Scott, if not in that of Jesus, but it is irrelevant. We remember these people only because they have significance in some context – a literary context in one case, a religious context in the other – and the context has virtually eclipsed their private individual beings.

Kierkegaard is sometimes criticized for his assertion, 'If the contemporary generation had left behind them nothing but these words, "We have believed that in such and such a year God appeared among us in the humble form of a servant, that he lived and taught in our community, and finally died", it would be more than enough. The contemporary generation would have done all that was necessary; for this little advertisement, this *nota bene* on a page of universal history, would be sufficient to afford an occasion for a successor, and the most voluminous account can in all eternity do nothing more."[7] Kierkegaard may be making his point in exaggerated form, but it is a salutary point against those who complain about our lack of information concerning Jesus. We are not interested in Jesus as an individual but as an event on a page of universal history, more precisely, as a moment in the history of faith – a decisive moment, Christians would say. But in acknowledging this, we are agreeing that the referend of the expression 'Jesus Christ' is not an individual human being, but this human being together with the community on which he made his impact; together with the descriptions which that community applied to him; together with many other factors which go to constitute the so-called 'Christ-event'.

The relation which the man Jesus bears to the Christ-event can be contrasted with other 'events' (the strangeness of the usage will become even more apparent) where the originating person is either better known or less well known that Jesus. For instance, we might consider the 'Homer-event' and the 'Hitler-event'.

We say, 'Homer is the author of *The Iliad*', and those who hold that 'The author of *The Iliad* is the author of *The Odyssey*' would go on to say, 'Homer is the author of *The Iliad* and *The Odyssey*.' Whether, as tradition avers, he was born in Smyrna or in one of eleven other cities that claim to be his birthplace, whether he was blind, and so on, are matters of little or no importance. On the other hand, whether there was one single author of the two great epic poems is a question of literary criticism that can be investigated and even answered with some degree of probability without reference to 'Homer' at all. The fact that we know very little of Homer as an individual does not prevent us from knowing a good deal about the Homer-event, and even from having some direct relation to it, in so far as these poems can still appeal to us and move us. Of course, we cannot doubt that there was at least one epic poet of outstanding genius at work in the Aegean area in the early part of the first millennium B.C. Whether one's understanding of the complex I have called the 'Homer-event' would be advanced by knowing the details of the life of 'Homer' is questionable.

On the other hand, if we consider the Hitler-event, this is something quite close to our own time, and we have a wealth of information about the individual after whom I have named the event. He was born on 20 April 1889 in Braunau-am-Inn, Austria; his father was a minor government official who had changed his name from Schicklgruber to Hitler; and so on. Older people still alive remember seeing him or hearing his speeches on radio, and even younger people can still see him on film. Biographers are able to reconstruct his life and to speculate on his psychological development. Yet even when this has been done with the greatest accuracy, we may feel that we are only skirting the Hitler-event, which is a complex arising out of German nationalism and militarism, certain strains of philosophy, the harsh provisions of the Treaty of Versailles, the collapse of the German economy, and so on and so on. In all this it could be argued that Hitler himself was no more than a symptom, a mediocre figure who happened to be thrown up by forces which he neither originated nor controlled. We may recall Tolstoy's belief, expounded in *War and Peace*, that the wars that had convulsed Europe a century before the time of Hitler were attributable to 'the mysterious forces that move humanity', and were not dependent on Napoleon who simply happened to be the focus for these forces. If this were the case with Napoleon, then it would be true *a fortiori* of Hitler.

It is convenient at this point to sum up the argument so far as it has gone. We are concerned with the question of the utility of the concept of a Christ-event for interpreting christological assertions. How far can such assertions, when they speak of 'Jesus Christ', be understood as referring not to an individual person but to a complex that is at once social, historical, and theological, and of which the individual person is one component, possibly the principal one? We have seen that significant figures of the past are known by interpretative descriptions, though where we still have some record of their words, the claim that there remains some knowledge by acquaintance cannot be ruled out. We have seen further that the use of descriptions takes us beyond the individual into a context of interpretative ideas, that is to say, into a 'world' in which the individual concerned made his impact and received his response. In some cases, such as Hitler, the biography of the individual remains accessible. In other cases, such as Homer, the individual has virtually vanished from sight. Jesus would come somewhere between these two.

It is tempting to the theologian to move his sights from the individual person, Jesus of Nazareth, to the complex event within which he belongs, for that might seem to compensate for the paucity of our historical knowledge about Jesus and allow us to say with Kierkegaard that, for theological purposes, we have more than enough. But then the difficulty in such a move would be that it might lead us to say about Jesus what we have already hinted about Hitler and even Napoleon – that the great man is only the more or less accidental focus of vast movements of the human spirit. Still, we might not be driven to say that, for there seems to be a creativity about the people to whom we refer as Jesus or Homer or Buddha which one does not associate with a Hitler or Napoleon.

Most of what I have been saying up till now has a fairly general character. It has been applicable not only to the Christ-event but to what I have called by analogy the Scott-event, the Homer-event, the Hitler-event, and so on. Now we must be more specific and concentrate attention on the Christ-event. Can we clarify what this expression means, and give it a more definite content?

I am not sure who introduced the Christ-event language into theological discussion. I suspect that it may have been Bultmann, for the expression is freely used in his writings, and it seems to have its widest currency among theologians who have been influenced by Bultmann, notably John Knox.

In Bultmann's own use of the event language, it seems to me that he stresses the term 'event' in order to get away from any objectification of Jesus Christ, from any supposedly static or abstract understanding of him as person or substance or nature or timeless ideal. Christ is the event of God's acting in the world, the bearer of the word; and since it is the word rather than its bearer that matters, the Christ-event is prolonged in all subsequent proclaiming of the word down to the present time. 'Jesus Christ is the eschatological event as the man Jesus of Nazareth and as the word which resounds in the mouths of those who preach him. . . . The formula "Christ is God" is false in every sense in which God is understood as an entity which can be objectified, whether it is understood in an Arian or Nicene, an orthodox or a literal sense. It is correct if "God" is understood here as the event of God's acting.'[8] In another writing, he says: 'If the proclamation of the word is a continuation of the Christ-event, then the conception as a whole leads to the affirmation that Christ is himself the word.'[9]

In Bultmann, the word is understood in its event character primarily as the word of preaching, and his interest is in the response of faith to this word on the part of the individual believer. Thus, although the Christ-event is extended through time, there is not much hint in Bultmann of its social character. But this side has been taken up by other exponents of the Christ-event idea, and is carried to considerable lengths in the writings of John Knox. He tells us that the 'event of Christ' includes 'the personality, life, and teaching of Jesus, the response of loyalty he awakened, his death, his resurrection, the receiving of the Spirit, the faith with which the Spirit was received, the coming into being of the Church'.[10] This is obviously a very complex reality indeed, but Knox makes it clear that within this complex it is the coming into being of the Church that has priority. He can say that 'the only adequate way to define the event is to identify it with the Church's beginning', or, again, that 'the event is the moment of the Church's beginning'. The beginning certainly included the more limited event of the career of Jesus of Nazareth, and Knox accords to that a normative value for the subsequent life of the Church, but 'the event has no historical reality except within the history of the Church'.[11]

Though Bultmann and Knox give somewhat different interpretations of the expression 'Christ-event', I do not think these are conflicting. It is rather that Knox fills out Bultmann at this point by taking more seriously the essentially social character of human existence. Both men are agreed in seeing the Christ-event as something larger than the career of the man Jesus of Nazareth, and both are agreed in making that larger reality the centre of faith. In that larger reality are joined inseparably the career of Jesus and its impact on the believing community, the history of Israel and the history of the Church, the tradition of the past and the present experience. These are inseparably joined because each flows into and penetrates the other. Jesus himself, like any other human being, does not exist apart from his relations to other human beings, and could not be isolated from them without mutilation. I think this way of looking at the matter does ease some theological problems, though it seems to give rise to others.

We have already seen that it does seem to ease the problem about the paucity and uncertainty of our knowledge about Jesus. If we think of Jesus and the community as together embraced in the Christ-event, then it would seem to be a matter of little or no consequence what is directly attributable to Jesus and what to the community. Whether, for instance, the so-called 'dominical' sacraments were instituted by Jesus or by his followers or whether both had a part in the matter, is a question of little consequence once it is acknowledged that there is no sharp dividing line between Jesus and the community, though in the past this question of dominical institution has sometimes been given theological weight. Even more importance was attached in some of the older books on Christology to the question of how Jesus understood himself. Did he think of himself as Messiah, or call himself Son of Man in some special sense? Did he first apply to himself the image of the Suffering Servant? Did he think of himself as standing in a unique relation to the Father? Or did some or all of these ways of thinking of him originate in the community? There can be no certain answers to these questions, and it may well be the case that their importance has been exaggerated, and that when one places Jesus in his context and acknowledges that he cannot be abstracted from his community or understood apart from the descriptions applied to him by the community, then such questions, although they continue to have a certain historical interest, do not appear to be of great theological moment.

Another problem which appears in a different light when we make the Christ-event rather than the individual Jesus the centre of Christology is incarnation itself. This too has often been considered in isolation, and we meet such speculative and far-fetched ideas as the implanting of the divine Logos in Jesus as an utterly unique event brought about by divine intervention. But if we think of Jesus in all his relationships, in his continuity with Israel on the one hand and with the new Christian community on the other, then it is within this complex human reality that God has come to expression in that new and fuller way that we call the incarnation. This was not just the work of a moment, but a process long preparing and then continuing – the coming into being of a new humanity. It is not just the formation of an individual (though there is no reason to doubt that Jesus is at the centre of it) but the creation of a new humanity, so that the wider community in which Jesus has his setting can be called his 'body' and even an extension of the incarnation. This way of thinking, which accords rather closely with the views of John Knox, provides a poss- ible answer to the objection of Dennis Nineham, that we do not have sufficient knowledge about the individual Jesus to claim that in him there emerged a new humanity.[12]

Still another issue that is illuminated is the notion of Christ's pre-existence. We have to see him in the closest connection with Israel and its expectations. We can say that Christ pre-existed in the sense that the Christ-event did not begin with the conception of the indi- vidual Jesus in the womb of Mary, but was already taking shape in the history of Israel, with its covenants and promises and expectations and images. Some theologians (and this would seem to be true of Bultmann) would similarly understand the post-existence (or risen life) of Jesus in the persistence of the kerygma and the unfolding of the new humanity in the life of the Christian community. I do not say that this is an adequate understanding of the risen Christ, but it does make some worthwhile contribution to the question.

But while one may concede that to understand the expression 'Jesus Christ' in this wider sense as the Christ-event does ease some of the questions that have vexed theologians, it would be idle to pretend that it does not raise new questions, or to deny that some of the old questions reappear in a new guise.

Thus, while it can be argued that questions about the historical Jesus appear less important if we stress his continuity with the com- munity that emerged into the light of history after the death of Jesus, and is still with us today, we then have to ask about the ground for our confidence that there is indeed this close continuity. We are assuming that Jesus and the community do constitute a unity (the Christ-event), so that the mind and words of Jesus are the mind and words of the community, and vice versa. This may be a fair assumption to make, and even quite sceptical scholars agree that it is most improbable that the general picture of Jesus presented in the New Testament will ever be falsified. Still, one cannot exclude the possibility of some discontinuity between Jesus and the community, a discontinuity due to misunderstanding, ignorance, or misrepresentation. This may mean then that the historical uncertainties surrounding the individual Jesus are not left behind when we turn from him to the Christ-event.

Again, in referring incarnation to the wider event and in talking of the Church as Christ's body and the extension of the incarnation, are we not taking altogether too grand and triumphalist a view of the Church, not only taking 'her teaching as his own', as Newman does in his hymn, but even identifying the quality of her life with his? This charge of overvaluing the Church is indeed one that has several times been urged against John Knox. We might reply that Christ is the Head and the Church his Body, thus claiming for him an originating and directing role in the emergence of the new humanity. Once again, we might believe that this is a claim with a good deal of inherent probability. But does not this claim entail that we must once more take up the task of distinguishing the individual Jesus from the penumbral event? One cannot escape the difficult question of how the continuity of Jesus and his community can be maintained, and how at the same time, in view of the manifest imperfections of the community, one can claim that Jesus Christ has brought God to decisive expression in the world.

Finally, I think it has also to be objected that those who speak of the Christ-event have left it too vague. Admittedly, one cannot set rigidly defined boundaries to any event, for one event merges into another, and there is a measure of arbitrariness in designating any area of happening as an 'event'. But to speak of the event as indefinitely prolonged into both past and future and as indefinitely extended through human society is to void the concept of recognizable content. Yet if it is to be theologically helpful, the concept of 'Christ-event' must have some measure of definition. Was there, for instance, a point at which the Christ-event could be said to have assumed its definitive shape? Where would that point be found – the closing of the canon of the New Testament, or the last of the ecumenical councils? Any answer would seem arbitrary, yet if we are to make use of the Christ-event idea, it needs to be given a more definite content than it has.

NOTES

1. Bertrand Russell, *Mysticism and Logic* (1918), pp. 209–32.
2. L. S. Stebbing, *A Modern Introduction to Logic* (1930), p. 26.
3. Walter Kasper, *Jesus the Christ*, tr. V. Green (1976), p. 37.

4. E. Schillebeeckx, *Jesus: An Experiment in Christology*, tr. H. Hoskins (1979), p. 479.
5. Hans Küng, *On Being a Christian*, tr. E. Quinn (1977), p. 547.
6. See my *God-Talk* (1978).
7. S. Kierkegaard, *Philosophical Fragments*, tr. D. F. Swenson (1936), p. 87.
8. Rudolf Bultmann, *Essays Philosophical and Theological*, tr. J. C. G. Greig (1955), pp. 286–7.
9. Rudolf Bultmann, *Faith and Understanding*, tr. L. P. Smith (1969), p. 308.
10. John Knox, *The Church and the Reality of Christ* (1962), p. 23.
11. Knox, op. cit., p. 22 and pp. 122–3.
12. Dennis Nineham in *The Myth of God Incarnate* (1977), p. 186.

8

Christology and Tradition

PETER HINCHLIFF

THERE is an obvious connection between Christian history and tradition, on the one hand, and the theological question about the divinity of Christ, on the other. Granted that the New Testament does not say, in so many words, that Jesus of Nazareth was actually God, it is natural to ask how the Christian Church came to assert that he was. That is an historical question. It may not be possible to provide an answer which is clear beyond doubt but, in principle, it is a question about what happened in the history of the Church – how and why did men and women come to believe this to be so? If the evidence can be obtained, the answer can be arrived at.

Whether Jesus *was* actually God and, if so, in what sense he was God is not, however, an historical question in the same sense.

That this is not immediately obvious is, at least partly, a result of the way in which the matter has been debated in the nineteenth and twentieth centuries. The question has repeatedly been put as a question about whether the *historical* Jesus of Nazareth and the divine Christ of classical theology are identical and that makes it seem as if the divinity of Christ is something which is detectable as a result of historical inquiry.

The question is, moreover, often put in a way that begs the question. Don Cupitt, for instance, wrote a brief article a few years ago which appeared under the headline 'The divine Christ – or the real Jesus?'[1] The immediate implication of such a heading clearly seemed to be that the 'real' Jesus could not be 'divine'. Then, as one read the article, further assumptions seemed to be made. The 'divine Christ' was contrasted not with the 'real Jesus', as in the title of the piece, but with the 'historical Jesus'. And the 'historical Jesus', it was implied, was the Jesus of the Synoptic Gospels. These suggestions seemed to add up to an assertion that it was possible to discover in the Synoptic Gospels an historical Jesus who was also the real Jesus and obviously not divine. And that, in turn, seemed to imply that an historical inquiry was capable of determining whether Jesus actually was God or not.

Now it cannot be certain, as James Barr has pointed out in his essay in this volume,[2] that the Jesus of the Synoptic Gospels is any more the 'real' Jesus than the Jesus of the Fourth Gospel or the Jesus of the Epistles. He can be called the 'historical' Jesus because he is the Jesus who appears in the historical sources – and Cupitt is clearly right to insist that those sources are of cardinal importance. But the most reliable of historical sources do not guarantee immediate access to absolute truth. No historian ever knows precisely how far a figure presented in his sources actually corresponds with the 'real' person. All one ever has – historically speaking – is other people's impressions of the real person. One is never in first-hand contact with the person himself. Even autobiographical sources are not reliable evidence for the 'real' person – and in the case of Jesus we do not have evidence of that kind.

The purpose of this rather laboured treatment of an obvious point is not merely to suggest that those who make much of the 'historical' Jesus of the Synoptic Gospels are themselves treading on uncertain ground. It is to point out that historical inquiry has its limitations. All it is capable of doing is to arrive at an *interpretation* of Jesus or the way in which people reacted to him. There is no guarantee that this is the real Jesus. Even supposing that it were possible to uncover with absolute certainty an exhaustive range of historical facts, it might still not be possible to give a definite answer to the question: 'Was Jesus of Nazareth actually God?' That is a theological question and not finally determinable by historical inquiry. Or, to put the question another way, supposing one had met Jesus of Nazareth, would one have known with any certainty whether he was actually God or not? It is extremely unlikely that there could have been any infallible test. One's answer would, in part, have depended on one's previous ideas about what God was like and partly upon one's reaction to the way Jesus behaved. It would be a judgement, an interpretation, a belief.

The question, 'Was Jesus of Nazareth actually God?' is a question about the 'real' Jesus. That is to say that the answer to it is of value only in so far as it corresponds to the truth about Jesus's being. But it is not a question which could ever be answered by historical inquiry or the amassing of historical facts. This does not mean that it is an improper question to ask, or that no answer can ever be given, or that historical inquiry is irrelevant to the answer. But it does mean that historical research is not going to provide the answer to theological or ontological questions.

A chemist presented with a bottle containing some substance or other can, by chemical analysis, tell one what the substance is. Chemical analysis of the contents of the bottle cannot, however, tell one who put the substance into the bottle. There are limits to chemical analysis and, in a sense, the usefulness of chemistry depends upon those limits for they arise out of the function which chemical analysis is designed to perform. One might nevertheless be anxious to know who had put the substance into the bottle if – let us suppose – one suspected that it had been used to commit a murder. Chemical analysis would tell one that the substance was poisonous. One would have to depend on other methods to determine who had put it there and thus discover the murderer.

In the christological issue, historical inquiry is similarly limited. It cannot answer the most important question, 'Was Jesus of Nazareth actually God?' At most it can only tell us whether other people judged, or believed, or interpreted his behaviour in this way.

So we are thrown back on the tradition and this is why, rightly, the argument is so often conducted in terms of what the historical sources say. But it is important not to go straight to the sources without perceiving the limitations to which historical inquiry is subject, so that one's expectations are realistic.

Even within these limitations, of course, a negative answer might be decisive. If, in the course of a murder investigation, chemical analysis proved that the contents of the suspect bottle were harmless, then knowing who put it there would become unimportant. If it were clear that the historical sources agreed in saying categorically that God was not present in Jesus of Nazareth in any special way, or if it proved that Jesus never existed, then the theological question might hold no further interest. But this, of course, is not the case. Not only do the earliest documentary sources – the Pauline Epistles – suggest that God was in Christ in a way which was so special as to be apparently unique but even the Synoptic Gospels contain passages which can at least be interpreted in this way. It is significant that Cupitt's article which I have been using as an Aunt Sally – unfairly, because it is, after all, a very brief piece and the heading may not even have been supplied by the author – admits that the case against the 'divine Christ' is not irresistible and is compelled to argue that '. . . Paul is still read far too much in terms of later "orthodoxy" '.

History or tradition seems to span the gap between the real Jesus and the divine Christ in some such way as this:

1. The real Jesus of Nazareth;
2. The impressions and beliefs of those who knew him in the flesh;
3. The oral tradition, developing first in a Jewish context;
4. The Pauline theological tradition;
5. Early christological traditions in Gentile Christianity;
6. The Synoptic Gospels;
7. The Fourth Gospel;
8. The Logos Christology;
9. Origen's eternal generation theology;
10. The Nicene formulary;
11. The Chalcedonian definition of the one person in two natures.

Obviously this is not an exhaustive list of every possible stage, nor can it be assumed that each stage neatly succeeds the previous one. But, broadly speaking, it would be generally recognized that there was some such process as this.

If most people would agree that this is *roughly* what happened, there is fierce disagreement about how the course of events is to be interpreted. Traditionally the 'orthodox' opinion has been that there was a proper and natural progress from the response to Christ on the part of his earliest disciples to the fully developed theology of the fifth century. The seeds of the latter were contained in the former and, though the divinity of Christ is not stated in the New Testament in terms of the hypostatic union of the two natures in the one person of the Logos, the fully developed Christology is no more than the logical dogmatic conclusion properly to be drawn from the scriptural foundations.

In its simple form this view is now difficult to maintain.[3] Many scholars would argue that the process is not so much a steady and natural development as a series of radically discontinuous stages.

Bernard Lonergan has attempted an account of patristic theology which describes the Nicene statement of Christ's divinity as both 'inevitable' and 'nonetheless new', so that he seems to stand between the 'continuous' and the 'discontinuous' schools of thought.[4]

Lonergan believes that the ascription to Christ of full divinity has less to do with a transition from Jewish to Greek thought than with what he calls 'dogmatic realism'. He distinguishes this dogmatic realism from 'naive realism' (which is a simple acceptance of what *appears* to be the case) and 'critical realism' (which requires rational inquiry before what is apparent is accepted as real). Dogmatic realists are realists in the sense that they are concerned with what is actually the case, but they are also dogmatic in the sense that they accept without question what is made known to them by revelation in the word of God. But because dogmatic realists are often unable to explain just why they believe what they do '. . . it can quite easily come about that, mixing naive realism with their dogmatic realism, they land themselves in inconsistency'.[5]

This inconsistency, Lonergan believes, is often to be found in the ante-Nicene Church. At Nicea, as a consequence of the various attempts to resolve the inconsistencies, there was a triumph for dogmatic realism. There was an implicit rejection of naive realism, '. . . a transition from things as related to us to things as they are in themselves, from the relational concepts of God as supreme agent, Creator, Omnipotent Lord of all, to an ontological conception of the divine substance itself. It marks no less a transition of the word of God as accommodated to particular people, at particular times, under particular circumstances, to the word of God as it is to be proclaimed to all people of all times under whatever circumstances – the transition from the prophetic oracle of Jahweh, the gospel as announced in Galilee, the apostolic preaching and the simple tradition of the Church, from all of these to Catholic dogma.'[6]

There are difficulties in this view, of course, difficulties about precisely what is meant by 'the word of God', how it is related to the words contained in the Bible and how the Bible is to be interpreted. There is something very Barthian about the way Lonergan talks about the word of God being 'Yes, Yes and No, No' and sometimes, as with Barth, one is left feeling a little unsure as to precisely what it would mean in practice. Nevertheless, there is something very attractive about such an approach. Lonergan seems to suggest that what was happening was a reaching through the naive realism of religious experience to the reality behind it. And here 'religious experience' would not simply mean subjective, personal religious experience (which Lonergan does not seem to regard as being very important in the proclamation of the truth) but the experience implicit in 'the prophetic oracle of Jahweh, the gospel as announced in Galilee, the apostolic preaching, and the simple tradition of the Church'. The movement is from God experienced or known as Creator, for instance, to God as he is and, presumably, from Christ as experienced as the activity of God to Christ as God understood ontologically. Lonergan seems to argue, in other words, that belief in the consubstantiality of the Father and the Son, however novel and revolutionary it may seem to have been, is no more than a necessary recognition of the reality implicit in what was apparent in Jesus Christ.

Those who take the view that the development of the doctrine was a series of radical and discontinuous stages are often inclined to suggest that each stage was a 'mistake' resulting from the transferring of an idea from one context to another. It is commonly argued that the title 'Son of God', given to Jesus by early Jewish Christians to signify his role as God's agent, acquired a new significance when used in Gentile circles, where tales about semi-divine beings were common, and finally came to be 'God the Son' of Nicene orthodoxy as an attempt was made to give a metaphysical account of what divine sonship must mean.

It has to be said that there is no actual evidence that this is what happened. Proponents of this view are more or less compelled to argue that because certain ideas were current in certain quarters, they *must* have been the cause of the various developments. Historically this is no more decisive than the kind of local history guidebook which continually says things like 'The young William Shakespeare *must* often have passed along this lane on his way to school.' In these sentences the word 'must' does not imply necessity: it merely means 'it is possible that'.

John Macquarrie, writing about Michael Goulder's contribution to *The Myth of God Incarnate*, was therefore justified in accusing him of falling into the 'genetic fallacy'[7] – the opinion that the existence of broadly similar ideas in the context within which a belief is born wholly accounts for that belief and proves it to be false.

Admittedly it is extremely difficult to see what evidence *could* be found to show that beliefs about Christ's divine nature had no other source than contemporary myths. Moreover those who, like C. F. D. Moule,[8] argue that the orthodox Christology is right because it is based on the reactions of those who actually knew Jesus, are relying upon an argument which is not totally unlike that of their opponents. It seems as though, at this point also, historical inquiry is unable to arrive at a conclusive answer.

A critic arguing that 'what is sauce for Goulder's "heretical" goose is sauce for Moule's "orthodox" gander',[9] has pointed out that both the evolutionary and the discontinuous theories about the origins of Christology are based on the same inadequate premise – the assumption that there was a single, homogeneous evaluation of Jesus among those who knew him and that this is contained in the New Testament. The truth is that a large part of the New Testament – the Pauline corpus, for instance – was written by people who never knew Jesus in the flesh. The documents seem to contain a number of different evaluations of Jesus's relationship with the Father. Those who encountered Jesus manifestly reacted to him in different ways. Apart from anything else there were those who judged him to be a blasphemer or possessed by an evil spirit. It is not, therefore, possible to appeal to some primitive, original, and unanimous opinion about Jesus, held by all those who knew him in the flesh, from which it can be said that later Christology developed either by a straightforward logical process or by a series of aberrations.

All this seems to suggest that any kind of belief, held even by the earliest Christians, about divine activity associated with Jesus of Nazareth was a matter of faith rather than something objective and external. Perhaps, even, Jesus's own understanding of himself and his relationship to the Father (whatever it was) was also more akin to the kind of knowledge we call faith than the kind of knowledge we have about ourselves by which we know that our parents were called John and Mary Smith.

This does not mean that historical inquiry is entirely irrelevant. How else should we ever have come to realize that there were varieties of early Christian beliefs about Jesus? But it does suggest that we have not taken seriously enough the relationship between history and faith and, perhaps, that we have concentrated too narrowly upon a particular period of history – the lifetime of Jesus of Nazareth.

Those who have argued that Christology developed by a series of radically discontinuous stages influenced by beliefs prevalent in contemporary cultures are not entirely agreed about the actual ideas which passed into Christianity by this syncretistic process. Frances Young, who believes that it was not a matter of one or two simple and obvious borrowings, but a 'tangled mass' of ideas, sums up the basic elements as follows:

i) The use of phrases like 'Son of God': such were undoubtedly current, though admittedly with a wide range of implications, and applied to both human and superhuman beings.

ii) The apotheosis or ascent of an exceptional man to the heavenly realm: we have been able to trace examples in both Greek and Jewish tradition. These two elements were brought together in the claim that Jesus was the Messiah – Son of God, risen from the dead and ascended to become God's 'right-hand man' in heaven.

iii) Belief in heavenly beings or intermediaries, some of whom might act as God's vicegerent in judgement at the end of the time; and the first of whom could have been God's instrument in creation. Once the risen Christ took his place in heaven, it is scarcely surprising that he ousted or demoted all these figures in the Christian imagination, while taking over many of their functions and thus becoming pre-existent.

iv) The fourth essential element is the idea of the manifestation of the chief of these heavenly beings on earth in a genuine incarnation. Given the combination of the first three elements, it seems the natural and logical outcome.[10]

But, Frances Young thinks, the natural outcome would most naturally produce a docetic Christ and that, given Christianity's 'inability to stray too far from the historical reality of Jesus of Nazareth', would not do. And so there was the problem of defining a Christology which would retain the historical reality while interpreting it 'according to the categories supplied by the supernatural speculations of the Graeco-Roman world'.

Not everyone would agree that this was a 'natural' process. It seems, in fact, a most extraordinary one. If what actually happened corresponds at all with this hypothesis, or others like it, then the 'real' Jesus of Nazareth attracted to himself while he was alive, and his memory continued to attract after he was dead, a whole complex of myths, beliefs, and ideas of an exceptional kind – and continued to do so for several generations covering at least a hundred years. Why should there be such a powerful drive to continue to develop beliefs and formulate them with such theological precision and rigour? For, though each of these ideas may possibly be parallel to others which existed at the time, or successively in various contexts, the accumulation of such a complex is without parallel. And if one really wanted clear historical proof that Jesus of Nazareth was unique, it is here. For no one else has been both so clearly an historical figure and, at the same time, the catalyst for the crystallizing of such a persistent, complex, and accumulating set of beliefs. There *must* have been some original reality – and here the 'must' does imply necessity, not mere possibility – to have provoked it. Heroic figures may become the focus of myth and legend. The Arthurian legends are examples of this kind of thing. One can understand why there should be a literary or a romantic interest in embroidering the tales. Insofar as the legends imply a quasi-religious belief in a once-and-future king, one can understand why there should be an interest in the propagation of that belief at certain periods in history. But, in spite of the glamour, the haunting tragic quality, the quasi-religious overtones, the possible political associations, the movement of the story from one cultural context into others, and the long history which it possessed, there was apparently no motivation sufficiently powerful and sustained to turn it into a serious, intellectually systematized, metaphysical foundation for a faith. Other historical figures have served as a focus for religious enthusiasm, a core round which myths have accumulated, or have founded new movements. But that someone so relatively obscure and unspectacular as Jesus was should have attracted so complex, vivid, and continuing a response – and one which so many great intellects thought it worth rendering in terms of metaphysics and theology – is itself part of his uniqueness.

Those who wish to attribute to Jesus a religious significance of some kind while attributing his 'divinity' to a series of mistakes, often identify the title 'Son of God' as the starting point from which the mistakes grew. Whether that title was used of Jesus in his own lifetime and, if so, what it would have meant in the context of first-century Palestine is a matter of historical inquiry to be settled by historians or New Testament scholars. It seems, indeed, to be thought increasingly likely that it *was* used – at least very soon after Jesus's death – though not as a title meant to imply that Jesus was himself actually God. So Geza Vermes, sympathetic but in no sense inclined to accept anything remotely like the Chalcedonian orthodoxy, believes that 'Son of God' was a popular title for Jesus derived '. . . from his activities as a miracle worker and exorcist, and from his own consciousness of an immediate and intimate contact with the Heavenly Father'.[11]

Even if this were all that could be said, it would nevertheless imply a good deal. First of all, the implication is that the title was used fairly widely by Jesus's contemporaries or near-contemporaries. Second, it is a title which has to do with his character and his activities (his 'person', that is to say). It was not simply a title given to someone who taught wisely or said inspiring things: it implied a certain attitude towards the kind of person he seemed to be. And the intimacy with the Father, which the title acknowledged, was not merely something which Jesus experienced subjectively. If the title was derived from it, it was something that could be observed and that in turn suggests that it was associated in the minds of observers with the actions he performed – exorcisms, healings, and so on. If Vermes is right, then, the title 'Son of God' was a way in which many (but not all) of those who encountered Jesus expressed their sense that God was 'at work' in and through Jesus (not merely present to him). Or – to put this in another way – there was already implicit in the use of the title a response of faith which saw Jesus as someone *by* whom God was revealed, not simply as someone *to* whom God was revealed.

In the Gospels it is in the accounts of the resurrection that Jesus is most obviously represented as a person by whom God was revealed. And this fact makes the resurrection narratives an embarrassment for those who wish to maintain that the real and the historical Jesus are the same thing and utterly distinct from the divine Christ. For there are no historical sources which 'go behind' the resurrection. It is there in both the Synoptic Gospels and the Pauline Epistles. It is part of the historical Jesus and if one wishes to argue that it is not part of the real Jesus one has to say that it could not really have happened because, after all, resurrections do not happen. This is not an *historical* argument, it is just an assertion that certain kinds of narrative are too unlikely to be true. But it does not provide one with an alternative access to some 'real' Jesus behind the story.

Of course, it is equally true that the resurrection is an embarrassment for those who wish to maintain the 'orthodox' Christology. Whereas the New Testament treats the resurrection as evidence for the fact that God was in Jesus in a unique and obvious way, much modern apologetic deals with it as a 'problem', something which has itself to be defended and which cannot therefore be used as evidence in support of other problematic assertions. So there is a tendency to leave the resurrection on one side while one tries to recover as much as possible of the 'divine Christ' from the rest of the Gospels.

Understandable though this is, it nevertheless diverts attention from certain crucial aspects of what the New Testament has to say – not so much about the Jesus of Nazareth but about the Jesus of Christian experience (to attempt to get away from the 'real Jesus'/'divine Christ' dichotomy). John 20.26–31, the appearance of Christ to Thomas, seems the most crucial passage of all. There seems to be widespread agreement that the Fourth Gospel is to be dated at about A.D. 90–100, the end of the first century. That would place it almost certainly after – yet not long after – the death of even a long-lived eye-witness of the crucifixion. It is, so to speak, the earliest date at which the Christian Church would have consisted entirely of those who had never actually met Jesus.

In one sense this is merely to say the kind of thing we were all told at Sunday School – 'As the apostles died off, it was realized that an effort must be made to preserve the tradition about Jesus and so the Gospels were written down.' But I am not concerned to make the point that the Fourth Gospel is preserving the historical truth about the historical Jesus in these verses. What seems to me important is very different. All those who have commented on John 20.28 (Theodore of Mopsuestia seems to have been the chief exception) seem to have agreed that 'My Lord and my God' is meant to be a statement of faith directed by Thomas to the risen Christ. Moreover virtually all modern commentators agree that the next three verses set out what ought to be the attitude towards Jesus of those Christians who have not actually seen him. So C. K. Barrett argues that the aorists in the Greek of verse 20 indicate that the Gospel was written at a time when the Church was composed of those who had not seen any resurrection appearances.[12] And Barnabas Lindars says, 'Being absent when Jesus appeared to his disciples on Easter night, Thomas was virtually in the position of the Christian who has not seen the risen Jesus and he should not have needed a further appearance in order to come to faith.'[13]

If these commentators are right, an important consequence follows. Whether the passage is, or is not, to be understood as a pseudo-prophecy falsely attributed to Christ, is not the vital question. What is important is that it ought to be seen as an attempt to put into words what it was actually like to believe in Christ, as a *present* reality, at that period of history when the Church had become a body of people who had not seen him in the flesh. The significance of this has been to some extent lost sight of because of the argument about 'real Jesus' or 'divine Christ'. Those on one side of the argument have taken the line that anything that happened as late as this has nothing to do with the 'real Jesus' and ought to be ignored. Those on the other side have been anxious to show that the later traditions preserved or at least did not misrepresent the 'real Jesus' and so have soft-pedalled the fact that the passage is really about Christian believing in subsequent generations.

Looked at in this latter light, however, the passage seems to say several important things. The faith of these Christians of later generations was directed at the *risen* Christ. It is thought of as a faith comparable with the faith of those who had actually seen Jesus. It is a faith which recognizes that the Jesus who manifests the power of God, is perhaps divine even in a 'metaphysical' sense.[14] Even if, again, one

90

leaves aside the question whether there is such a 'metaphysical' or ontological implication, it is clear that the evangelist is making an extraordinary claim. He is saying in effect that it is possible for a Christian who has never seen Jesus to be related to God through Jesus in the same way as those who knew him in the flesh. This relationship is not represented as being simply a matter of obeying the teachings of Jesus but of experiencing a 'life' mediated through him. Presumably the evangelist is himself claiming to have had this experience of a relationship with God mediated through Jesus.

What is important about this is what might be called the permanent or continuing significance of Jesus. That can sound like a pious but rather meaningless phrase, but it is actually a very striking one when one thinks about it. For the syncretistic hypothesis, like that of Frances Young, ought to try to offer some explanation of *why* – in this case alone – a miracle-working Hasid should, after his death, have gone on attracting to himself an accumulating complex of associations to such an extent that within two or three generations he should have come to be regarded as God in the flesh. It cannot be said that such a process was natural or necessary ('it *must* have happened'). It did not happen – nothing remotely like it happened – in any other case. But the documents *do* purport to offer an explanation and that explanation deserves serious consideration simply because it is part of the earliest source material we have.

The explanation offered is that Jesus has a continuing or permanent significance. He had an extraordinary effect in his own lifetime, not on everybody but on those who responded to him with faith. That led to his being called 'Son of God', perhaps even before the crucifixion, in an attempt to express the belief that God was manifested in his actions. But these things continued to happen afterwards. Those who had known him in the flesh claimed to be able to communicate their experience of him, of the kind of person he was and of their sense that he was God's agent. And those to whom they communicated these things claimed to be able to make the same response of faith and to have the same sense that their relationship with God was mediated through Jesus.[15] They regarded Jesus not just as an agent of God's power and activity in the past but as a present reality and therefore as having a continuing, permanent, possibly eternal significance. This is why the account of the faith of later generations is focused on the risen Christ, not on an historical Jesus now dead and confined to a particular period in history.

This is not just one of those 'it-must-have-been' hypotheses, for there is actual evidence – not just the Fourth Gospel but notably, of course, St Paul himself. For here again the debate about 'real Jesus' or 'divine Christ' has diverted attention from the main point. The advocates of the 'real Jesus' dismiss Paul as one of the villains responsible for inventing the 'divine Christ'. The advocates of the 'divine Christ' try to show that Paul was not inventing but was carrying on the tradition. In fact what was happening was that Paul, who never knew Jesus in the flesh however much he may have learnt about him from the tradition, nevertheless believed that the crucified and risen Jesus lived in him.[16] Whether he was justified in that belief may be open to question. What is not open to question is that *that* is what he believed. The evidence is there.

The uniqueness of Jesus does not simply rest, in other words, upon the character of the historical person (which may not be fully recoverable) but upon the undoubted fact that all this 'mythology' grouped itself around the historical person. Moreover it appeared to be vindicated by the further fact that the claim that the faith was communicable seemed to be borne out in the experience of subsequent generations.

Two points need to be made very clearly at this stage.

First: I am not claiming that any of this *proves* that the Christian gospel is true or that Jesus is divine. The experience claimed by Paul and others may have been a delusion or it may have had nothing at all to do with *Christ*. But it is evidence for why they said what they did about Jesus. It sprang from their experience and there is no need to indulge in 'must have beens'.

Second: the word 'experience' needs some explanation. I do not mean that every Christian had a Damascus road conversion experience such as Paul's. Then as now, people seem to have come to believe in Jesus Christ in different ways and their 'experience' of him was of different kinds. By 'experience' I mean simply that they do not seem to have thought of Jesus – as they might have thought of Isaiah or Jeremiah or John the Baptist – as a prophetic figure through whom God had worked powerfully but who was now shut away in a past era. He was somehow a present reality, a focus for their religious experience, a means of making sense of life, and a source of the strength by which to live it. All this need not have been (and clearly it has not always been) a highly emotional, 'felt' experience. It has been said that what characterizes a religious response to the nature of human existence '. . . is not merely that one who makes it thereby finds some way of coming to terms with the world's contingency. Rather it is that one who thus responds feels himself to have a source of security that does not come from himself or from anything in the world'.[17] If this is fair, then it could be said that Christians found a way of coming to terms with the world's contingency by taking as their pattern the way in which the historical Jesus had come to terms with it himself. In so doing they found that they had access (or so they believed) to a source of security that came from something real, present, and continuing. Their religious response (faith) was related to both an historical person and a present reality and they believed the two to be identical.

Claims of this kind do not, of course, cease with the sub-apostolic age. St Cyprian, in what I think is the earliest personal account of baptism as subjectively experienced, says: '. . . then in a wonderful way what had been doubtful became sure, what had been hidden was revealed, what had been dark was lit up, what had seemed difficult before could now be attempted, what had been thought impossible was now able to be done'.[18] That was in the middle of the third century. At the other end of Africa and in the fourth decade of the nineteenth century, at a meeting of Namaqua Christians, amid a number of long testimonies full of quotations from the Authorized Version, expressions of conventional piety, and condemnations of beer-drinking, one convert used a spontaneous phrase to describe his faith in Jesus Christ. It was, he said, 'a pillow on which to rest'.[19] And so one might go on quoting examples to show the various ways in which this sense of Christ as a present reality has been expressed. An evangelical might describe it as '. . . a personal acceptance of the reality of Christ somehow alive in his people now'.[20] Monsignor Ronald Knox put it like this: 'Our whole life now is Christ-conditioned, he is the medium in which we exist, the air we breathe; all our nature is summed up, all our activities are given supernatural play in him.'[21] All these people, in very different ways, seem to be saying the same thing – that Christ for them is still 'Son of God', in the sense that he is the agent through whom divine power is manifested and the medium (to avoid saying 'mediator') through whom God is known.

It is essential to realize that the importance of this tradition within the Church (or, at least, its relevance to Christology) is not that in itself it proves that Christ is God, or demonstrates the necessity of a 'felt' conversion experience or that it provides the *content* of an under-standing of Christ's nature. Its significance lies simply in the *fact* of its existence. But if it witnesses to something real then it gives the title 'Son of God', in Vermes's sense, a new significance. One is saying that Jesus is *still* the kind of person for whom the title is appropriate and that means that he must *be* a kind of person who transcends time. The fact of Christian experience is part of the material out of which Christology has to be constructed. To say that it is not a legitimate part of that material is to say that it is not a legitimate part of Christianity. And while, of course, that might be the case, the experience is so ingrained a part of the tradition that one would need a watertight case before it could be declared improper or illegitimate.

One could make the same point in a slightly different way by asking the question: 'What would have to be "ontologically" the case about Jesus for the "experience" to be not merely a delusion?'

It might be held, of course, that there is no real need to go beyond the two basic points – the historical Jesus to whom the title 'Son of God' was given in this undefined sense and the subsequent experience of later generations of Christians. It would seem that at first no such need was felt. But

> In later times the church, no longer perceiving the power and decisiveness of the agent–son model, felt it necessary to go considerably further in the direction of a metaphysical identity between Jesus and his heavenly father. In the last few years it has come to be questioned whether this whole construction of an incarnate God is either credible or intelligible today . . . the earliest Christians were under constraint to stop considerably short of this: but by acknowledging Jesus to be son of God they were able to say all they needed about his divine authority and power. . . .[22]

While this is almost certainly true, it is a position that it would only have been possible for the earliest Christians to adopt so long as they were not asked any further questions. Sooner or later the questions would be asked and answers would have to be given – 'What does this actually amount to?' 'What is the reality behind what is apparent and apparently experienced?' 'Is Jesus still Son of God now?' 'If so, what does that say about his reality?' Lonergan is right in maintaining that theology has to say what it believes to be the actual case, not what people *feel*. And this is why it was so important to stress earlier that it was the *fact* of continuing Christian 'experience' rather than its *content* which was part of the data on which Christology was built. The Church may rightly insist upon the validity of the experience: it has been part of the tradition from the beginning. But it would clearly be impossible to allow that every subjective experience that anyone claimed to have had must be treated as equally valid. Nor could every such experience be allowed to count as information about God or about Christ. Theology, quite as much as historical inquiry, can claim to test the validity of the *content* of experience.[23]

But the *fact* of the experience, if it is admitted to be real and not an illusion, is a different matter. Jesus of Nazareth merited the title 'Son of God' in his lifetime because he was the agent of divine activity and God was manifested through him. If he is still such an agent, then his 'sonship' seems to have a permanence, an *ontological* character, quite different from that of prophets or other inspired persons. It seems to belong to his nature rather than to have come upon him intermittently and from outside.

He was first given the title 'Son of God', perhaps, in a sense very different from the Chalcedonian two-natures definition. But that title ascribed to him a relationship with God which actually said something about God as well as about Jesus of Nazareth; about God's involvement with his creation and his concern for it which were manifest in Jesus. If he could be thought of as manifesting the nature of God so directly, and if that manifestation was not limited to a period or periods of time, then he possessed a unique relationship with the Father. The *uniqueness* of that sonship seemed to become more apparent in the experience of subsequent generations of Christians, and, though it might have been easier if questions about defining his nature or his place in a metaphysical hierarchy of being had not been asked, it is difficult to see how they could have been evaded for ever. Once the question was asked, the permanence and continuity of Jesus's role as Son of God was bound to mean that the answer would be given in ontological and metaphysical terms.

In a sense this is to say that history is not enough. If one is going to give an explanation at all one has to go beyond the historical inquiry about how Jesus seemed to those who met him in the flesh. One has to attempt to say what one believes him actually to be. Given the metaphysical framework within which Christian theology operated in the fourth and fifth centuries, there does seem to be a kind of inevitability about the way in which the other options were closed off and the Chalcedonian definition of Christ's person emerged. The terms in which it was expressed are now probably neither helpful nor significant to most Christians. But this does not mean that the whole issue can simply be shelved. For those for whom Jesus of Nazareth continues to be the core and focus of their belief, whose religious experience is not associated with some abstract notion of God but with the person of Jesus as the agent of divine activity, there is still a necessity to say who and what he is. And so the search for the right language in which to do it, goes on.

NOTES

1. In *The Times*, 17 September 1977.
2. See above, pp. 17–18.
3. Because Roman Catholic scholarship has only been relatively recently exposed to the problems inherent in such a view, it is instructive and helpful to see how these are faced by essentially orthodox but open-minded Roman Catholic theologians, e.g., K. Rahner and W. Thüsing, *A New Christology* (1980).
4. *The Way to Nicea* (1976), p. 136.
5. Ibid., p. 132.
6. Ibid., pp. 135ff.
7. 'Christianity without incarnation? Some critical comments', in M. Green (ed.), *The Truth of God Incarnate* (1977), p. 141.
8. C. F. D. Moule, *The Origins of Christology* (1977), p. 3.

9. J. Moulder, 'Some questions about the origins of Christology', *Journal of Theology for Southern Africa*, no. 30, March 1980, p. 51. This is an important and stimulating article and, although I had written a first draft of this essay before reading it, I am much indebted to it.
10. F. Young, 'Two Roots or a Tangled Mass', in *The Myth of God Incarnate*, pp. 118ff.
11. G. Vermes, *Jesus the Jew* (1973), p. 211.
12. C. K. Barrett, *The Gospel According to St John* (1955), p. 477.
13. B. Lindars, *The Gospel of John*, New Century Bible (1972), p. 616.
14. See C. K. Barrett, op. cit., p. 460 (who plainly regards this as a good thing) and G. Vermes, op. cit., p. 212 (who does not).
15. This is a point missed by J. Moulder, op. cit., p. 50 when he compares Paul's experience of Christ and Cicero's religious experience. The point is not whether it is possible to judge which is better, or more intense, or more real. The really significant thing is that Paul associated his religious experience with *Christ*, a human, historical person.
16. Cf. J. Moulder, op. cit., pp. 40ff.
17. C. Lyas, 'The Groundlessness of Religious Belief', *Reason and Religion*, ed. S. C. Brown (1977), p. 174.
18. *Ad Donatum*, iv, somewhat paraphrased.
19. Archives of Methodist Missionary Society, Cape and Albany, Box VI, file 1829–33: 'The substance of speeches made at Lily Fountain, 17 October 1833, by natives at their missionary meeting' – a printed report.
20. J. Poulton, *A Today Sort of Evangelism* (1972), p. 63.
21. R.A. Knox, *The Hidden Stream* (1952), p. 91.
22. A. E. Harvey, *Jesus and the Constraints of History* (forthcoming), ch. 7.
23. See P. T. Geach, *Truth, Love and Immortality* (1979), p. 33, for reasons why it is not possible to '. . . get away from the business of assent to dogmatic propositions, and think rather in terms of loving trust in a Person'. And cf. S. W. Sykes on the differences between Barth and Schleiermacher in S. W. Sykes (ed.), *Karl Barth: Studies of his Theological Methods* (1979), pp. 29ff.

9

*A Sermon**

PETER BAELZ

Preached in Durham Cathedral on Christmas Day 1980

John 1.14: And the word became flesh

What should a preacher do on Christmas Day?

Should he simply let the Christmas story speak for itself, as in the traditional service of nine lessons and carols? Or should he rehearse it again in his own words, setting forth the great wonder of the Saviour's birth in Bethlehem, foretold by prophets, announced by angels, signified by a star, celebrated by shepherds and wise men?

The preacher must surely attempt something more. It is right that in his sermon he should invite us to reflect upon the Christmas story and to consider how we may appropriate its meaning for ourselves.

So far, so good. Before such reflection can begin, however, an urgent question demands to be heard. 'Is the story true?'

> And is it true? And is it true,
>   This most tremendous tale of all,
> Seen in a stained-glass window's hue,
>   A Baby in an ox's stall?
> The Maker of the stars and sea
> Become a child on earth for me?
>
> And is it true? For if it is,
>   No loving fingers tying strings
> Around those tissued fripperies,
>   The sweet and silly Christmas things,
> Bath salts and inexpensive scent
> And hideous tie so kindly meant,
>
> No love that in a family dwells,
>   No carolling in frosty air,
> Nor all the steeple-shaking bells
>   Can with this single Truth compare –
> That God was Man in Palestine . . .'[1]

---

*For reasons why the final chapter takes this form, see above (Preface, p. viii).

Is the story true? Or is it only a work of pious fiction, belonging to the world of make-believe rather than that of truth and reality? Do men and angels really converse together? Do stars really guide the wandering wayfarer? Was Jesus really born of a virgin in Bethlehem of Judaea? Did God really become man?

If the story is pious fiction, no doubt it remains, and always will remain, a lovely and captivating tale. Nevertheless, it will be no more than a story, a 'fair fancy' of the kind which Hardy sang about:

> Christmas Eve, and twelve of the clock.
>   'Now they are all on their knees',
> An elder said as we sat in a flock
>   By the embers in hearthside ease.
>
> We pictured the meek mild creatures where
>   They dwelt in their strawy pen,
> Nor did it occur to one of us there
>   To doubt they were kneeling then.
>
> So fair a fancy few would weave
>   In these years! Yet, I feel,
> If someone said on Christmas Eve,
>   'Come; see the oxen kneel
>
> 'In the lonely barton by yonder coomb
>   Our childhood used to know',
> I should go with him in the gloom,
>   Hoping it might be so.[2]

Hoping it might be so! But knowing it would not be so! A fair fancy, but a false fancy nonetheless.

When today we listen once again to the Christmas story, children of our own doubting age as we inevitably are, the same nagging and persistent question troubles our minds. Can it really be true?

Let me confess straightaway that I find myself more at home with the beginnings of the Gospel as recorded by Mark and John than as recorded by Matthew and Luke.

Mark commences his Gospel with an account of Jesus's baptism by John. At his baptism Jesus is designated Son of God. Immediately he begins his ministry in Galilee, proclaiming the Kingdom of God and calling men to repent. All that happens before his baptism, including his birth, is passed over in silence. It has no special significance for this Gospel writer. It was his living and his dying, rather than the manner of his birth, which marked Jesus out from other men.

John – the perceptive, meditative John – also commences his Gospel with the Baptist. In a preceding introduction, however, in which he suggests the significance of what is to follow, this Gospel

98

writer traces the coming of Jesus back into eternity, to the express will of God, to his word in the beginning. In Jesus, in this one man, at this particular moment in history, the divine light is focused and the divine word uttered. Indeed, it is more than uttered. It is also enacted in flesh and blood. Such, for John, is the message and truth of the incarnation. The details of the birth, the how and the where and the when, are of no consequence. No angels, no star, no shepherds, no wise men, no virgin mother. Only the word become flesh.

When Matthew and Luke in their turn tell of the coming of Jesus, the Saviour, they offer us stories of his birth. For so wonderful a person there must have been a wonderful birth. Stories of that birth no doubt circulated among the early Christian communities. The Jewish Scriptures were searched for clues concerning how it must have been. We cannot rule out in this process the work of pious fiction. This fiction, however, was intended to illuminate the fact – the fact of the coming of the Son of God, of the word become flesh.

But is it fact? Dare we affirm the truth of the incarnation without basing it necessarily on the stories surrounding Jesus's birth? May we in all honesty believe in the word become flesh? Why should we believe? Why should anyone believe?

When we take account of the origins of the Christian Church, reconstructing them as far as we can with the tools of historical inquiry, we find that centuries of argument and debate occurred before it was generally agreed how we might most appropriately speak of Jesus. The evidence to hand was not only the teaching and life of Jesus himself. It was also his dying, and especially the significance which his dying acquired in the light of experience of his risen power and presence. His disciples not only remembered their master, they also went forth to preach and to live in his name. Thus with experience and reflection they became convinced that in Jesus God had become man, not merely because others had told them that it was so, but also because of their own discovery of what Jesus had done for them and of what he was now doing in them and through them for others. What was that?

We may express it at first in well-known words from the Scriptures. 'God has visited and redeemed his people.' 'God was in Christ, reconciling the world to himself.' But we must also try to express it in our own way, not because we can guarantee to do it any better, but in order that we may all hear the gospel each in his own language.

In and through Jesus a bridge has been built between things as they are and things as they are meant to be. In our ordinary experience fact and value mostly fall apart. Things are not as we believe they ought to be. What we know to be good and desirable all too easily eludes our grasp. We live in a fallen world. We ourselves are broken and divided people. Jesus, however, has brought us in himself the promise and foretaste of wholeness and life. In him the broken is mended, divisions are healed, and creation begins anew. He gives us real, ultimate grounds for confidence and hope.

The gospel proclaims the reconciliation of Creator and creature, of God and man, of time and eternity – a reconciliation that will be brought to fulfilment because in Jesus it has already been established. The gospel offers us more than a teaching to be obeyed, it offers us also a life to be shared. Jesus himself is more than a teacher come from God, he is also a life-giver communicating to us the divine life.

Belief in the incarnation is belief that it is in Jesus himself that God has grounded the work of man's salvation. It is through this man's life, received, shaped, completed, and shared, that God has communicated to us his own life. Thus the birth, and the life, and the death, and the consequences which flow from them for all mankind, in the divine economy belong together.

> All this was a long time ago, I remember,
> And I would do it again, but set down
> This set down
> This: were we led all that way for
> Birth or Death? There was a Birth, certainly,
> We had evidence and no doubt. I had seen birth and death,
> But had thought they were different; this Birth was
> Hard and bitter agony for us, like Death, our death.[3]

Birth and death are both parts of a single pattern of life. What is grasped by Eliot's Magi is also grasped by Auden's Mary:

> Dream. In human dreams earth ascends to Heaven
> Where no one need pray nor ever feel alone.
> In your first few hours of life here, O have you
> Chosen already what death must be your own?
> How soon will you start on the Sorrowful Way?[4]

How soon will the baby start on the sorrowful way? There is a single pattern of love in creation and redemption, the pattern of self-giving and sacrifice. The history of Jesus is one with the history of God. The Father sends his Son, and the Son does the will of his Father. But the story does not end there. For it is also God's gracious will that the same history should embrace the history of mankind, your history and my history.

The Christmas story of the babe in the manger, of angels and shepherds and wise men, has a kind of truth of its own, even if in its details it is only a 'fair fancy'. Children both young and old respond to it at a deep level of human consciousness. It touches their feelings and awakens their dreams. They find in it the expression of their profoundest hopes and fears. It speaks of a lost innocence, of a world of good will, of peace and joy.

But is this the only 'truth' that Christmas celebrates? Is there nothing apart from the symbolic expression of human hopes and fears? Is there no word from God?

The Christmas gospel proclaims, above and beyond all our hopes and fears, that the word has in Jesus become flesh, and that he is for us today, in his living presence, what he was for his disciples of old, the life and love of God.

In order to recognize this truth and make it our own we need the creative imagination which enables us to discern beneath the surface confusion the deeper pattern of things. We also need the critical intellect to assure us that we have not lost touch with the world of experience. Intellect without imagination, drawing solely on the consistencies of the past, is bound by existing horizons and insensitive to the possibility of the radically new. Imagination without intellect loses touch with fact and confuses the possible with the actual.

If we are to recognize and appropriate the truth of the incarnation we need, beyond both imagination and intellect, a heart of love. We cannot test the truth of the incarnation without ourselves risking the adventure of love. The gospel is not only *about* the love of God for man; it is that love expressed and offered to man. Therefore it can be known only as it is received. If, then, we find ourselves strangely moved by the Christmas story, it may not be just because in the Christ child our own dreams, our own hopes and fears, find their perfect expression. It may also be that our lives are touched by the self-effacing love of God, and that the living Christ calls us to wonder and to worship.

How was Jesus born? Where was he born? When was he born? I do not know. But when I reflect on his teaching, his life, his death, and his continuing presence, and when I find myself responding, however inadequately, to a love that seems to know no bounds, I am prompted to say with all the strength that love, imagination, and intellect can provide, that this is truly God's Son, his word become flesh. To walk with him is to walk humbly with God.

If we believe this to be true, as the gospel invites us to believe that it is true; if in Jesus Christ God and man are truly one; if he is the Way, the Truth, the Life; then may we not in fair fancy go again this Christmastide to Bethlehem, to see the thing that has come to pass, and to join our songs with those of angels, and to worship with shepherds and wise men, while a mother watches over her baby in a manger? And shall we not perceive there the very humility and love of God himself?

Peter Baelz

NOTES

1. John Betjeman, *Christmas*.
2. Thomas Hardy, *The Oxen*.
3. T. S. Eliot, *The Journey of the Magi*.
4. W. H. Auden, *At the Manger*.

Index

Alcestis 35
aletheia 24
Anna Karenina 36
Anselm 32
archaeology 49–50

Archimedes 25
art, and truth 29 ff
Arthurian legends 88
Assumption, doctrine of 10
Auden, W. H. 100

Barbour, R. S. 54
Barrett, C. K. 90
Betjeman, John 100
biography 56
Buddhism 8
Bultmann, R. 12, 30, 43, 76–7

certainty 44f
Chalcedonian definition 2, 32, 83
Christ, see Jesus
Christ-event 28, 31, 58, 69ff
Christian Scientists 10
Christology 1, 24ff, 52ff, 67–8, 72, 83ff
Coleridge, S. T. 40–1
crucifixion 48, 50–1
Cupitt, D. 81
Cyprian 93

Dead Sea Scrolls 2, 48, 81ff
development of doctrine 84–5
dissimilarity, criterion of 46–7, 56
divinity of Christ 2, 81ff

Elijah 60
Eliot, T. S. 100
Elisha 60

Ford, D. F. 23
form-criticism 42ff, 55–6
Frei, H. 23

Gadamer, H.-G. 29ff
Galileans 61
Geach, P. T. 96
Gnosticism 5
Göttergeschichte 19
gospel 27
Gospel of John 16, 30, 38, 39, 48, 51, 83, 90, 98
Gospel of Mark 39, 45, 56, 98
gospels, apocryphal 44
gospels and history 34, 43ff, 59ff
Goulder, M. 86
Green, M. 9

Habakkuk Commentary 58
Hanina ben Dosa 59
Hardy, Thomas 98
Harvey, A. E. 17, 94
Hasid, Hasidim 64, 91
Heidegger, M. 25, 29
Hercules 35
Hick, J. 2
Hitler 74–5
Homer 30, 74

Ignatius of Antioch 5
imitatio Dei 65–6
incarnation, doctrine of 22, 78
'inwardness' 25
Islam 8

Jesus
    as exorcist 60
    as prophet 47, 61
    as teacher 60–1
    his pre-existence 78
    his son-ship 64–5
    his theocentric piety 62
    facts about 49–50
    'real' 81–3, 90
    see also divinity of Christ,
        Messiahship, Son of God

103

Index

Kähler, M. 30
Kasper, W. 72
kenosis 3
Kierkegaard, S. 25f, 31, 73ff
Kingdom of God 63ff
Kirk, G. S. 20
Knowledge by acquaintance, by
  description 69ff
Knox, J. 76ff
Knox, R. 93
Küng, H. 7, 73

Lampe, G. W. H. 4
Lindars, B. 90
Lonergan, B. 25, 32, 84–5, 94
Lucas, J. 24
Lyas, C. 96

MacKinnon, D. 32
Macquarrie, J. 86
messiahship 22, 53, 56, 67
miracles 49, 60
Mormons 10
Moulder, J. 96
Moule, C. F. D. 86
myth 9, 18ff
Myth of God Incarnate 1, 9, 36, 52, 86
'mythos' 40

Namaqua 93
names, proper 69ff
Napoleon 75
narrative theology 5, 12
Nazareth 48
Neill, S. 8
Newman, J. H. 79
Newton, I. 25
Nicea 84
Nineham, D. E. 54, 78

'odd is true' 46–7
omen 36
Origen 83

parousia 57–8
Pastoral Epistles 12, 26
Paul 11, 56–7, 59, 62, 83, 91–2
Pharisees 61

Philo of Byblos 21
Pilgrim's Progress 37
Poulton, J. 96
prophet, Jesus as 47, 49–50, 61–2

Qumran, *see* Dead Sea Scrolls

Rahner, K. 95
Reimarus, H. 28
resurrection 4, 35–6
Robinson, J. A. T. 3
Russell, Bertrand 69ff

Schillebeeckx, E. 72
Scott, Walter 72
Scripture, authority of 10–11
Segal, J. B. 68
Shakespeare 35, 40
Smart, N. 13
Son of God 2, 53, 67, 88–9, 94
Spirit, and Christology 4
Stebbing, S. 70
Story, and Christology 6ff
story, biblical 14ff
Strauss, D. F. 28
Sykes, S. W. 9, 23, 33, 96
symbol 36

Temple, W. 9
Theodore of Mopsuestia 90
Thucyclides 7
Thüsing, W. 95
Tillich, P. 32
Tolstoy 35
truth, imaginative 38ff
truth, in christology 24ff
Truth of God Incarnate 8, 95
truth, of stories 6–7

Vermes, G. 88–9

War and Peace 6, 18
Wellhausen, J. 55
Wiles, M. 42, 51
'Word', the 76

Young, F. 87, 91